THE FIRST BOOK OF MACCABEES

D1096934

THE FIRST BOOK OF
MACCABEES

COMMENTARY BY H. A. Fischel

SCHOCKEN BOOKS/NEW YORK

First published by Schocken Books 1948
10 9 8 7 6 5 4 3 2   85 86 87 88
Copyright © 1948 by Schocken Books Inc.

Library of Congress Cataloging in Publication Data
Bible. O.T. Apocrypha. Maccabees, 1st. English. 1985.
   The first book of Maccabees.
   Originally published in 1948.
   "Follows the text contained in The Aprocrypha and
Pseudepigrapha of the Old Testament in English,
translated by W. O. E. Oesterley, edited by R. H. Charles,
and published by the Clarendon Press, Oxford, 1913"—P.
   1. Bible. O.T. Apocrypha. Maccabees, 1st—
Commentaries. I. Fischel, Henry A. (Henry Albert),
1913–   . II. Title.
BS1823.F5 1985   229'.73077   85-2458

Manufactured in the United States of America
ISBN 0-8052-0793-7

Contents

PUBLISHER'S NOTE   7

INTRODUCTION   9

THE FIRST BOOK OF MACCABEES

Alexander's Conquests and Legacy   19

The Spread of Hellenism in Judaea   20

Judaea a Base for Antiochus' Egyptian Expeditions   21

Despotic Centralization and Religious Persecution   24

The Start of the Maccabaean Uprising under Mattathias   26

Judah's Initial Progress   33

The First Major Successes   36

The Restitution of the Traditional Worship in Jerusalem   43

Violent Pagan Reaction and Maccabaean Counter-
measures   46

Death of Antiochus   54

Reverses and Compromises   56

Another Maccabaean War   60

The Treaty with the Romans   65

Defeat and Death of Judah   69

Jonathan's Succession and Early Struggles   72

Jonathan's Aid to a Syrian Revolution   77

Jonathan's Statesmanship in the Wars for the Syrian
Throne   87

Jonathan's Successful Foreign Policy   94

Progress toward National Sovereignty under Simon   99

Simon's Exalted Rank at Home and Abroad   105

New Clashes with Syria   111

Simon's End and John's Accession   117

CHRONOLOGY   121

MAPS   122

Publisher's Note

THE English translation of the First Book of Maccabees
follows the text contained in The Apocrypha and Pseudepigrapha of the Old Testament in English, translated
by W. O. E. Oesterley, edited by R. H. Charles, and
published by the Clarendon Press, Oxford, 1913. The
permission by the publishers to use this translation is
gratefully acknowledged.

New section titles have been given the translation;
the transcription of a number of names and terms and
text interpolations have in certain instances been
changed.

Introduction

THE First Book of Maccabees is a simple historical record, lucid and straightforward. The locale of the events described in it is a comparatively undeveloped hinterland — Judea; the scenery is rural; the events are dwarfed by the more spectacular ones of the period; yet, like a prism, First Maccabees reflects the decisive world-historical and cultural developments of the age. Though a book full of cruel warfare and political intrigue, it is nevertheless permeated by a longing for peace and stability. While partial and partisan, it is yet ennobled by its unwavering stand against tyranny and superior material power, and by its insistence on the sovereign rights of traditional culture. Though focused on historical detail, it also witnesses to the power of prayer, martyrdom, and the good name. It is therefore more than a mere historical pageant.

The Maccabean revolt is set against a vivid and fascinating background: the grandiose attempt of the Hellenistic age to create a world-encompassing culture. It is the age of the struggles between Macedonia, Syria, and Egypt (323–146 B.C.E.), the successor states of the empire of Alexander the Great (336–323). The last stage of this period sees the decline and final conquest of these states by the heirs of Hellas and the Orient: Rome in the West, Parthia in the East (146–30). Scholars who ordinarily hesitate to compare historical periods nevertheless emphasize the surprising similarity of the Hellenistic period with our modern era.

It was an age of ever widening horizons, of international traffic and trade, of voyages and discoveries from

Britain to Singapore. The Ancient World was passing from economy in kind to a money economy. From Spain to India there developed, along with the growing cosmopolitan populations, a highly refined city culture ushering in a new epoch in art, science, and entertainment, and producing new types of diplomacy, administration, and warfare. The material civilization of Greece had spread everywhere. Greek pottery and theaters, Greek legal contracts, were as ubiquitous then as tin cans, newspapers, and moving-picture houses are today. Even at that early period, in the words of J. B. Bury, "sophistication . . . the craving for sensation, the credulous attraction to the occult," were characteristics of urban life.

Not unlike our present age it was a time of great tension and unsolved problems. Slavery, famine, oppressive taxation, and the yawning gulf between rich and poor begot social conflicts. The age is therefore characterized by continuous struggle, frequently culminating in upheavals and civil war. Throughout the period, the harshness of the various systems of vassalage and serfdom was somewhat mitigated by the pressure of increasingly emancipated or desperate populations on states already hard-pressed by constant warfare. The less Hellenized countryside and its towns steadily improved their status in face of the innumerable Grecized cities founded by Hellenistic potentates, and the cities, in turn, successfully strove for greater freedom from their royal overlords. Democracy clashed with tyranny, cosmopolitan ideals with racial exclusiveness, rationalism in religion with crude paganism, materialism with a mystical yearning for immortality, sensuality with asceticism. Not only women of royal birth, such as the Macedonian Olympias, the Jewish Salome Alexandra, and the Egyptian Cleopatra, but those of common origin as well enjoyed a

higher degree of freedom than was ever dreamed of before.

There was widespread resistance to some of the more
oppressive aspects of Hellenism, such as taxation, the
spoliation of temples, grain speculation, and military
service. This resistance was successful to a considerable
degree in Syria, where the Seleucids steadily weakened
under the double onslaught of Rome and Parthia. Oriental cultures were thus able to maintain themselves
against the Greek-Macedonian civilization. In order to
placate native sentiment, local cults and temple states
were granted freedom, and even financial support. Antiochus Epiphanes, frequently misrepresented as a fanati-
cal protagonist of Hellenism, favored Samaritans and
Phoenicians, and initiated a revival of Babylonian culture. It may be — we cannot be sure — that Antiochus
set up a Semitic pagan cult in the Jerusalem sanctuary,
and not a Hellenic one; and the Chaldean garb of the
biblical Book of Daniel written in 165 may have been
inspired by Antiochus' futile gesture — as Nebuchad-
nezzar *redivivus* — toward the ancient Orient.

Though less accessible and important than the coastal
plain (Philistia and Phoenicia), the Judean hill country
was inescapably drawn into these larger developments,
first under the Egyptian Ptolemies (300–200 B.C.E.),
and later under the Syrian Seleucids (200–129). The
Maccabean revolt in a sense is to be considered as part
of the Oriental renaissance in the later phase of Hellenism. It is in line with the successful attempts at sovereignty on the part of Pergamum, Babylonia, and some
Greek cities and native kingdoms of Asia Minor. Historical "necessity," however, can in no way minimize
the impressiveness of the Jewish struggle for freedom.
Neither can historical parallels overshadow the grandeur

of some of the Maccabean leaders, who acted in a situation which offered no more than a slim chance of success.

In some respects the Jewish struggle for freedom was unique. The attempt, as a military or punitive measure, to annihilate a traditional religion was made only in Judea, and it was only there a bitter civil war ensued over the question of religious allegiance. The existence of a pro-Egyptian party — Judea until a short time previous had been under Ptolemaic rule — and her strategical importance as a border province, aggravated an already precarious situation. Furthermore, Jewish monotheism, with its absolute ethical and religious codes, inspired in its adherents a sincerity and tenacity which made this rebellion more important and fruitful than any other similar revolt. In addition, the Jewish tradition of theological history-writing perpetuated the fervor and aspirations of this struggle, making them felt throughout the later Jewish generations and throughout the entire history of the Judeo-Christian civilization. When writing his Roman history, Livy enviously observed that Greek history had gained its fame not so much by the greatness of its heroes as by the greatness of its historians. The same thing might be said of the historians of the Maccabean uprising — the anonymous authors of Daniel and First and Second Maccabees as well as Jason of Cyrene and Josephus Flavius.

It was not so much the fault of these writers as that of modern historians that the Maccabean revolt was overdramatized as a conflict between the Greek and Jewish spirits. In their most valuable achievements, Hellas and Judea had certainly much in common. The best of Hellenistic thought was tending toward a form of monotheism. Both possessed a lofty system of ethics and held to the belief that history was a meaningful process. Both taught hatred of tyranny, the nobility of poverty, and the virtue of self-discipline. Wherever Judaism and Hellenism encountered each other under favorable conditions, a fruitful amalgamation soon ensued. Rabbinical thought and Christianity might, aphoristically, be called Hellenized Judaism (and Hellenism, orientalized Greek culture). At any rate, Jewish law in its later form, Jewish mysticism in its various shades, the religious philosophy of Philo, the Midrash, and the medieval Jewish thinkers — all these are unintelligible without an appreciation of the influence of Hellenism. In the first century c.e., and possibly earlier, the educated traditional Jew of Palestine included Greek in his studies, and in the Middle Ages, Plato and Aristotle were greatly revered names among Jews.

The real source of conflict lay elsewhere: in the cruder forms of Hellenism, in its pagan and secular aspects, and above all, in the political ambitions which utilized it. The core of the conflict was a fight for religious freedom and national survival, the true antagonist being a political totalitarianism which employed enforced cultural uniformity as its tool. The Maccabees thus fought against oppression, arrogance, and paganism as such, rather than against the essentials of Hellenism. The antagonist merely wore the garb of the Hellenist.

The results of the struggle bear this out. The immediate gains were freedom of religious practice, the customary rights of a sanctuary, greater political independence, and territorial acquisitions. But these very achievements drew Judea into the orbit of city culture — it engaged in trade, its princes kept a lavish court; it developed a diplomacy, an army, and embarked on a policy of defensive aggressiveness — all characteristic of the Hellenistic state. The names, literary tastes, and observances even of the most pious of Israel were soon to bear the imprint of the Hellenistic age.

First Maccabees is only one among a considerable number of literary works produced by the great emotional upsurge of the second century B.C.E. If we follow those who maintain that some of the biblical Psalms were written in the wake of the Maccabean renaissance, we can find in this literature a whole range of passions corresponding to the passions roused by the events of Maccabean times. The civil wars and persecutions are reflected in laments (Pss. 44; 74; 79; 83), as well as in the mysterious, half-gloomy, half-reassuring atmosphere of the historico-theological apocalypse (parts of Daniel, Enoch, the Assumption of Moses); in homage to the Law (wisdom and "testament" literature); in the love of Zion (Pss. 125; 129); in the glorification of the martyr (II Maccabees, Martyrdom of Isaiah, and other midrashic folklore); and in the spirit of resistance (in the moral "novels" [see 1:6]). Victory, on the other hand, is reflected in exultation (Pss. 118; 149) and gratitude (Pss. 46–48; 76; *et al.*), and in tribute to the victorious dynasty (Pss. 2; 110) — reaching its apotheosis in the following century (Testament of Levi). The chronicle-like matter-of-fact history of First Maccabees is apparently without parallel; Second Maccabees approximates the novel rather than history. With some of the Maccabean Psalms and with the novels, our book shares a striking characteristic: it is anonymous, nor does it pretend to have been written by one of the great prophets of the past, as did most of the works of contemporary pseudepigraphic literature.

The unknown author of our book wrote in the time of victory, when national enthusiasm ran high, probably under John Hyrcanus, 135–104 B.C.E. (see 13:53). The small temple state of Jerusalem, re-established with Persian permission by Jewish exiles from Babylon in 538 B.C.E., was now, under a new high-priestly dynasty, a

sizable territory within Palestine. It is therefore under-
standable that the author's admiration for the Hasmoneans is complete and undivided. In view of the deadly
fight for survival, just barely won, his feelings against
the pagan oppressors and the rival Jewish party can
hardly be expected to show much objectivity. In black-
and-white fashion he contrasts good with evil, Israel
with the nations, Jew with pagan. And yet, perhaps
under the influence of Israel's prophetic teachings, he
does not suppress mention of Jewish and pagan complaints against some of the Maccabean measures (11:
4ff.). His traditional piety is also evident in his emphasis
on absolute obedience to the Torah, in his eschewing of
any mention of the divine name, and in his conviction
that "those who trust in the Lord will not perish."

Our author wrote in Hebrew, frequently following the
Bible's literary example, particularly in the case of its
historical narrative, its lives of the Jewish kings, and its
occasional interludes of Psalm and prayer. The Greek
version, incorporated in the Septuagint, and the English version based on it, faithfully preserve many of the
Hebraisms and the biblical flavor of the lost original.
The author must have been an eyewitness or at least a
contemporary of those eventful days, and must have had
access to the documents of the Maccabean archives, perhaps as the royal chronicler. His report is thus fairly accurate, and in many instances preferable to the parallel
works of Second Maccabees, Josephus, and the classical
historians.

Later Jewish tradition, judging more soberly, and
perhaps, more religiously, did not share the author's enthusiasm for the Hasmonean dynasty. The pious in Israel withdrew from the victorious party at an early date,
as soon as the immediate aim of religious freedom was

achieved. The rabbis must have recognized in the early Maccabees the first traces of that Hasmonean tyranny which they later condemned (not Hellenism as such, for Plato's philosopher-king or a true Stoic on the Jewish throne might have been acceptable to them).

For this reason Hanukkah became not a glorification of the Hasmoneans, but a festival of thanksgiving (see 4:59). Partly because of this hostility to the Hasmoneans, and partly because of their late origin, the four books of Maccabees were not included in the canon of Holy Scriptures of Judaism; they were relegated to the Apocrypha, the "hidden" or excluded books.

To the early Church, however, the Maccabees and their adherents, by their readiness for martyrdom (see II Macc. 7), were saints, and their books canonical. For Protestantism they became the glorious pattern of the struggles of true religion, and their books acquired the semi-canonical status of the rest of the Apocrypha. Such poets, artists, and composers as Raphael, Handel, Calderon, and Longfellow made them the subject of their work.

At the same time the stern criticism that later Judaism made of the Hasmonean rule has also grown in significance. What we have here is no mere academic issue: to this day these two opposing points of view continue to exercise their influence on the minds and hearts of men.   H.A.F.

THE FIRST BOOK OF MACCABEES

Alexander's Conquests and Legacy

And it came to pass after Alexander, the son of Philip 1
the Macedonian, who came from the land of Chittim,
had smitten Darius, king of the Persians and Medes,
that he reigned in his stead. And he waged many wars, 2
and won strongholds, and slew kings, and pressed forward to the ends of the earth, and took spoils from many 3
peoples. But when the land was silenced before him, he
became exalted and his heart was lifted up. Then he 4
gathered together a very mighty army, and ruled over
lands and peoples and principalities; and they became
tributary unto him.

And after these things he took to his bed, and perceived 5
that he was about to die. Then he called his chief minis- 6
ters, men who had been brought up with him from his
youth, and divided his kingdom among them while he
was yet alive. And Alexander had reigned twelve years 7
when he died. And his ministers ruled, each in his par- 8
ticular domain. And after he was dead they all assumed 9
the diadem, and their sons after them for many years.
And these wrought much evil on the earth.

[1] The book appropriately opens with the greatest event of antiquity: the conquests of *Alexander* the Great, 336–323 B.C.E.

Chittim is a biblical term for greater Greece.

Darius III Codammanus, 336–330 B.C.E.

[3] *the ends of the earth:* Alexander's empire reached from the
Danube to the Indus, i.e. included almost all of civilized Europe
and the Middle East.

[9] Alexander's successors waged costly wars against each other.

The Spread of Hellenism in Judaea

¹⁰ And a sinful shoot came forth from them, Antiochus
Epiphanes, the son of Antiochus the king, who had been
a hostage in Rome, and had become king in the one hun-
¹¹ dred and thirty-seventh year of the Greek kingdom. In
those days there came forth out of Israel lawless men,
and persuaded many, saying: 'Let us go and make a
covenant with the nations that are round about us; for
since we separated ourselves from them many evils have
¹² come upon us.' And the saying appeared good in their
¹³ eyes; and as certain of the people were eager to carry
this out, they went to the king, and he gave them au-
¹⁴ thority to introduce the customs of the Gentiles. And
they built a gymnasium in Jerusalem according to the
¹⁵ manner of the Gentiles. They also submitted themselves
to uncircumcision, and repudiated the holy covenant;

[10] *Antiochus* IV Theos *Epiphanes* ("God manifest"), soon
parodied into "Epimanes" ("madman"), *son of Antiochus* III,
reigned from 176–163 B.C.E.

a hostage in Rome: Antiochus Epiphanes was kept in Rome
for twelve years after the decisive defeat of Syria at Magnesia,
190 B.C.E.

*the one hundred and thirty-seventh year of the Greek King-
dom,* i.e. according to the Seleucid Era (S.E.), which began on
the accession of Seleucus I of Syria, October 1, 312 B.C.E. It corresponds to 176/175 B.C.E. In most cases, the author of First Maccabees counted the Seleucid Era from the first of Nisan, 311
B.C.E.

[11] *lawless men:* the party of the collaborationist Hellenizers.
These "modernists" saw in traditional religion the cause of Israel's misfortunes. The traditionalist party, however, saw in the
Law "glory," "beauty," and the aim of life (2:12f.). Oppression
was to them a transitory evil.

yea, they joined themselves to the Gentiles, and sold themselves to do evil.

Judaea a Base for Antiochus' Egyptian Expeditions

And when, in the opinion of Antiochus, the kingdom was [16] established, he determined to exercise dominion also over the land of Egypt, in order that he might rule over two kingdoms. So he pushed forward into Egypt with an [17] immense force; with chariots, and elephants and horsemen, together with a great fleet. And he waged war [18] against Ptolemy, the king of Egypt. And Ptolemy turned back before him, and fled; and there fell many wounded. And they captured the fortified cities in Egypt; and he [19] took the spoils from the land of Egypt.

And Antiochus, after he had smitten Egypt, returned in [20] the one hundred and forty-third year, and went up

[14] *gymnasium:* a stadium for athletic exercises in the nude. It was the center of Greek social life and a requirement for Hellenistic citizenship.

[15] *uncircumcision:* a painful operation which concealed circumcision and thereby silenced the derision of the pagans. It was tantamount to abandoning Judaism, which was understood as a *holy covenant* between God and his people.

[17] A legal dispute over the possession of Palestine preceded this war, the seventh between Egypt and Syria within a century.

[18] *Ptolemy* VI Philometor, 181–146 B.C.E.

[19] In the end, however, Egyptian resistance flared up again, and Antiochus unsuccessfully besieged Alexandria. The ensuing events have to be seen in the light of this failure. Greek traditions try to justify Antiochus' measures by pre-dating an uprising of the pro-Egyptian Jewish party (Judea was an Egyptian province from 320–200 B.C.E).

[20] *143* S.E. = 169 B.C.E.

21 against Israel and Jerusalem with a great army. And in
   his arrogance he entered into the sanctuary, and took
22 the golden altar, and the candlesticks for the light, and
   all its accessories, and the table of the shewbread, and
   the cups, and the bowls, and the golden censers, and the
   veil, and the crowns, and the golden adornment on the
23 façade of the Temple, and he scaled it all off. Moreover,
   he took the silver, and the gold, and the choice vessels;
24 he also took the hidden treasures which he found. And
   having taken everything, he returned to his own land.

25 'And there was great mourning in Israel in every place;
26 And the rulers and elders groaned;
   Virgins and young men languished,
   And the beauty of the women faded away;
27 Every bridegroom took up his lament,
   She that sat in the bridal-chamber mourned.
28 And the land was moved for her inhabitants,
   And all the house of Jacob was clothed with shame.'

29 After the lapse of two years the king sent a chief collector of tribute to the cities of Judah; and he came to
30 Jerusalem with a great host. And he spoke unto them
   peaceful words in subtilty, so that they had confidence

[21] Temple robbery was a crime also according to pagan ethics
and was frequently referred to in Hellenistic political propa-
ganda. On the stolen objects see Exod. 30:1ff. (altar); 25:31ff.
(candlestick); 25:23ff. (table); 26:31ff. (veil). — Antiochus IV
was in arrears with his payments of the Roman tribute, imposed
on his father, Antiochus III, after Magnesia (1:10).

[25–28] A fine specimen of a popular elegy in the biblical style.
We do not know whether our author himself wrote the poetical
parts of First Maccabees or whether he incorporated contemporary poetry into his work.

[29] According to II Macc. 5:24, his name was Appolonius. The

in him; but he fell upon the city suddenly, and smote it
with a grievous stroke, and destroyed much people in
Israel. And he took the spoils of the city, and burned it 31
with fire, and pulled down the houses thereof and the
walls thereof round about. And they led captive the 32
women and the children, and took possession of the cattle. And they fortified the city of David with a great 33
and strong wall with strong towers, so that it was made
into a citadel for them. And they placed there a sinful 34
nation, lawless men; and they strengthened themselves
therein. And they stored up there arms and provisions, 35
and collecting together the spoils of Jerusalem, they laid
them up there. And it became a sore menace, for it was 36
a place to lie in wait in against the sanctuary, and an evil
adversary to Israel continually.

And they shed innocent blood on every side of the 37
    sanctuary,
And they defiled the sanctuary.
And because of them the inhabitants of Jerusalem fled, 38
And she became a dwelling for strangers,
Being herself estranged to her offspring,
And her children forsook her.
Her sanctuary became desolate as a wilderness,   39

office of "chief collector of taxes" (minister of finance) was —
under various names — a very high one in the Hellenistic state.

On account of Roman intervention, Antiochus was forced to
evacuate Egypt in spite of his victory in a second campaign. In
Jerusalem, the high priest Menelaus, installed by Antiochus, had
been expelled by his predecessor Jason, an act which Antiochus
considered an open revolt (II Macc. 5: 5ff.). — Judea was then
transformed into a bulwark of defense against Egypt.

[30] We learn from II Macc. 5: 25f. that this incident happened
on a Sabbath, on which observant Jews did not take up arms.

[33] This *citadel,* called Acra, manned by a Syrian garrison, over-

Her feasts were turned into mourning,

Her sabbaths into shame,

Her honor into contempt.

⁴⁰ According as her glory had been so was now her dishonor
increased,

And her high estate was turned to mourning.

Despotic Centralization
and Religious Persecution

⁴¹ And the king wrote unto his whole kingdom, that all
⁴² should be one people, and that every one should give up
his religious usages. And all the nations acquiesced in ac-
⁴³ cordance with the command of the king. And many in
Israel took delight in his form of worship, and they be-
⁴⁴ gan sacrificing to idols, and profaned the sabbath. Furthermore, the king sent letters by the hand of messengers
to Jerusalem and to the cities of Judah that they should
⁴⁵ practise customs foreign to the land, and that they
should cease the whole burnt offerings, and sacrifices,
and drink offerings in the sanctuary, and that they
⁴⁶ should profane the sabbaths and feasts, and pollute the
⁴⁷ sanctuary and those who had been sanctified; that they
should build high places, and sacred groves, and shrines
for idols, and that they should sacrifice swine and other

shadowed the Temple and dominated Jerusalem. The *city of
David* was the name of one of Jerusalem's heights. According to
the Jewish historian Flavius Josephus (born 37 C.E.), the Acra
was leveled after the Maccabean wars of independence.

[41] Internal revolts and the growing strength of Rome led
Antiochus to centralize certain aspects of law and cult in some
parts of his empire. Although the decree is hardly genuine, nevertheless, it vaguely reflects a true historical situation. Nowhere,
however, was his new policy more cruel than in Judea, since here
his reforms were simultaneously punitive measures, partly insti-
gated by the influential Jewish Hellenists.

unclean animals; and that they should leave their sons [48] uncircumcised, and make themselves abominable by means of everything that was unclean and profane, so [49] that they might forget the Law, and change all the traditional ordinances. And whosoever should not act according to the word of the king, should die. In this manner did he write unto the whole of his kingdom; and he [51] appointed overseers over all the people; and he commanded the cities of Judah to sacrifice, every one of them. And many of the people joined themselves unto [52] them, all those who had forsaken the Law; these did evil in the land, and caused Israel to hide in all manner of [53] hiding-places.

And on the fifteenth day of Kislev in the one hundred [54] and forty-fifth year they set up upon the altar an 'abomination of desolation,' and in the cities of Judah on every side they established high-places; and they offered sacri- [55] fice at the doors of the houses and in the streets. And the [56] books of the Law which they found they rent in pieces and burned them in the fire. And with whomsoever was [57] found a book of the covenant, and if he was found consenting unto the Law, such an one was, according to the king's sentence, condemned to death. Thus did they in [58] their might to the Israelites who were found month by

[46] *high places:* altar mounds.

[47] The pig was sacred in Greek religion to certain deities of the earth (of fertility).

[54] *Kislev,* December; *145* s.e. = 167 b.c.e.
  The profaning *abomination of desolation* (from Dan. 12:11) was a pagan altar in the form of the ancient sacred stone. Statues of Zeus, possibly bearing the likeness of the king, may have been displayed in the courts of the Temple.

[55] Romans and Greeks offered sacrifices in the porch to the protective deities of the house.

59 month in their cities. And on the twenty-fifth day of the
month they sacrificed upon the altar which was upon the
60 altar of burnt-offering. And, according to the decree,
they put to death the women who had circumcised their
61 children, hanging their babes round their necks, and they
put to death their families, together with those who had
62 circumcised them. Nevertheless many in Israel stood
firm and determined in their hearts that they would not
63 eat unclean things, and chose rather to die so that they
might not be defiled with meats, thereby profaning the
64 holy covenant; and they did die. And exceeding great
wrath came upon Israel.

The Start of the Maccabaean
Uprising under Mattathias

1 In those days rose up Mattathias, the son of John, the   1
son of Simon, a priest of the sons of Joarib, from Jerusa-

[61] The heroism of women became a prominent subject in the
Jewish literature of that time (Esther; Judith; Susanna; the
mother of the seven martyred sons, II Macc. 7).

[62f.] Daniel (Dan. 1:8) and Judith (Jud. 12:2) acted similarly. Defilement was caused by the consumption of (1) unclean
animals, (2) blood generally (strictly prohibited in the Penta-
teuch), and (3) the sacrificial meat of idol worship.

[64] According to the Jewish belief of the time, it was God's
wrath directed against Israel because of sin (corruption of individual and society) which caused persecution. Nevertheless, suf-
ferings were considered as a gift of mercy, since they not only
atoned for sin, but also led to repentance and new strength (II
Macc. 6:12ff.; 7:33), and precipitated the downfall of the agent
of punishment through his haughtiness and presumptuousness.
Even the tragic side of human history was meaningful (see 3:8).

[1] *Mattathias* appears in later Jewish tradition as a high priest
(main prayer on Hanukkah, Targum Song of Songs). — The name
of an older ancestor, Asamonaios (Heb., Hashmon), gave rise to
the appellation "Hasmoneans" for the Maccabean family (Josephus).

lem; and he dwelt at Modin. And he had five sons: 2
John, who was surnamed Gaddis; Simon, who was 3
called Thassis; Judah, who was called Maccabaeus; 4
Eleazar, who was called Auaran; and Jonathan, who was 5
called Aphphus.

And he saw the blasphemous things that were done in 6
Judah and in Jerusalem, and said, 'Woe is me, why was 7
I born to behold the ruin of my people and the ruin of
the holy city, and to sit still there while it was being
given into the hands of enemies, and the sanctuary into
the hands of strangers?'

Her house is become like a man dishonoured;   8
Her glorious vessels are carried away captive;   9
Her infants have been slain in her streets,
Her young men with the sword of the enemy;
What nation hath the kingdom not taken possession of, 10
Of what nation hath it not seized the spoils?
Her adornment hath all been taken away,   11

the sons of Joarib (or Jehoiarib) were one of twenty-four classes of priests (I Chron. 24:7). Flavius Josephus came from the same distinguished family.

Modin or Modein is the present El-Medije, east of Lud (Lydda).

[2] *John,* from the Heb. Yohanan. *Gaddi,* Heb. (see Num. 13:11), corresponds to Felix ("the happy one").

[3] *Thassis,* the "zealous," or Tharsis (Syriac version), the "leader," "counselor" (see v.65).

[4] *Judah:* the Greek form is Judas. — *Maccabaeus* (Maccabee); probably "hammerer," or "extinguisher." Later tradition interpreted this surname as an acrostic for the Heb. equivalent of "Who is like unto Thee among the mighty, O Lord" (Exod. 15:11).

[5] *Auaran* or Avaran, probably the "piercer" (see 6:43ff.). — *Aphphus,* the "cunning." — The five brothers acquired these by-names by reason of their virtues.

[6] *He* refers to Mattathias.

Instead of a free woman she is become a slave.

12 And behold, our holy things, and our beauty, and our glory have been laid waste,

13 And the heathen have profaned them! To what purpose should we continue to live?

14 And Mattathias and his sons rent their garments and covered themselves with sackcloth, and mourned greatly.

15 And the king's officers who were enforcing the apostasy
16 came to the city of Modin to make them sacrifice. And many from Israel went unto them; but Mattathias and
17 his sons gathered themselves together. Then the king's officers answered and spake unto Mattathias, saying: 'A ruler art thou, and illustrious and great in this city,
18 and upheld by sons and brothers. Do thou, therefore, come first, and carry out the king's command, as all the nations have done, and all the people of Judah, and they that have remained in Jerusalem; then shalt thou and thy house be numbered among the friends of the king, and thou and thy sons shall be honoured with silver and
19 gold, and with many gifts.' Thereupon Mattathias answered and said with a loud voice: 'If all the nations that are within the king's dominions obey him by forsaking, every one of them, the worship of their fathers, and have
20 chosen for themselves to follow his commands, yet will I and my sons and my brethren walk in the covenant of
21 our fathers. Heaven forbid that we should forsake the

[18] *Do thou . . . come first.* The townspeople would have followed the example of their leading citizen.

[19] *forsaking . . . the worship of their fathers.* Pagan religious feeling permitted the change or addition of gods, since none was believed absolute.

[26] *Phinehas* and Elijah (v.58), often thought of as one person, gained great fame on account of their *zeal* for the survival of

Law and the ordinances; the law of the king we will not [22] obey by departing from our worship either to the right hand or to the left.' And as he ceased speaking these [23] words, a Jew came forward in the sight of all to sacrifice upon the altar in accordance with the king's command. And when Mattathias saw it, his zeal was kindled, and [24] his heart quivered, and his indignation burst forth for judgement, so that he ran and slew him on the altar; and at the same time he also killed the king's officer who [25] had come to enforce the sacrificing, pulled down the altar, and thus showed his zeal for the Law, just as [26] Phinehas had done in the case of Zimri the son of Salom. And Mattathias cried out with a loud voice in the city, [27] saying, 'Let everyone that is zealous for the Law and that would maintain the covenant come forth after me!' And he and his sons fled unto the mountains, and left all [28] that they possessed in the city.

At that time many who were seeking righteousness and [29] judgement went down to the wilderness to abide there, they and their sons, and their wives, and their cattle; [30] for misfortunes fell hardly upon them. And it was re- [31] ported to the king's officers and to the troops that were in Jerusalem, the city of David, that men who had set at nought the king's command had gone down into hiding-places in the wilderness. And many ran after them, and [32] having overtaken them, they encamped against them, and set the battle in array against them on the Sabbath

Judaism (Num. 25 : 7f. and Palestinian Targum thereon; I Kings 18), attacking the seducers of the people.

[27] *Let everyone . . . come forth.* This may have been one of the original slogans of the uprising.

[29] *to the wilderness,* where one could live in freedom as a no-mad, defy aggressors, who were at a great disadvantage, and render considerable damage to the royal power (loss of taxes).

³³ day. And they said unto them: 'Let it suffice now; come
forth, and do according to the command of the king, and
³⁴ ye shall live.' And they answered, 'We will not come
forth, nor will we do according to the command of the
³⁵ king, and thereby profane the Sabbath day.' Thereupon
³⁶ they immediately attacked them. But they answered
them not, nor did they cast a stone at them, nor even
³⁷ block up their hiding-places, saying, 'Let us all die in
our innocency; Heaven and earth bear us witness that
³⁸ ye destroy us wrongfully.' And they attacked them on
the Sabbath; and they died, they and their wives, and
their children, and their cattle, about a thousand souls.

³⁹ And when Mattathias and his friends knew it they
⁴⁰ mourned greatly for them. And one said to another, 'If
we all do as our brethren have done, and do not fight
against the Gentiles for our lives and our ordinances,
⁴¹ they will soon destroy us from off the earth.' And they
took counsel on that day, saying, 'Whosoever attacketh
us on the Sabbath day, let us fight against him, that we
may not in any case all die, as our brethren died in their
⁴² hiding-places.' Then were there gathered unto them a
company of the Hasidim, mighty men of Israel who
willingly offered themselves for the Law, every one of

[38] The cowardly attack on the Sabbath had been first employed by Ptolemy I of Egypt when he seized Jerusalem in 320
B.C.E.: See also II Macc. 15 : 1ff.

[42] *Hasidim* (the "pious") : a group distinguished by their strict
adherence to the tradition.

[44] The author is carried away by his enthusiasm and falls un-
consciously into poetic diction, using the biblical "parallelism of
sentences."

The Maccabean party meted out punishment to isolated Syro-
Grecian units (*sons of pride*, see II Sam. 3 : 34) as well as to the
Jewish renegade.

them. And all they that fled from the evils were added 43
unto them, and reinforced them. And they mustered a 44
host, and smote sinners in their anger, and lawless men
in their wrath; and the rest fled to the Gentiles to save
themselves. And Mattathias and his friends went round 45
about, and pulled down altars, and they circumcised by 46
force the children that were uncircumcised, as many as
they found within the borders of Israel. And they pur- 47
sued after the sons of pride, and the work prospered in
their hand. And they rescued the Law out of the hand of 48
the Gentiles, and out of the hand of the kings, neither
suffered they the sinner to triumph.

And the days drew near that Mattathias should die, and 49
he said unto his sons: 'Now have pride and rebuke
gotten strength and a season of destruction and wrath
of indignation. And now children, be zealous for the 50
Law, and give your lives for the covenant of your
fathers. And call to mind the deeds of the fathers which 51
they did in their generations, that ye may receive great
glory and an everlasting name. Was not Abraham found 52
faithful in temptation, and it was reckoned unto him for
righteousness? Joseph, in the time of his distress, kept 53
the commandment, and became lord of Egypt. Phinehas, 54

[51] *an everlasting name.* This would seem to sum up one of
the principal beliefs in immortality of that time; the eternal
glory of the good name.

[52ff.] The meritorious deeds of the forefathers played an important role in the piety of the time (e.g., Sir. 44ff.; Pss. 99; 105;
the liturgy for fast days). The references are to Isaac's "sacrifice"
(Gen. 22), *Joseph's* courage in prison (Gen. 39: 9), *Joshua's* obedience to the divine command (Num. 27: 18ff.; Josh. 1: 2ff.),
Caleb's faithful report (Num. 13: 30ff.), *David's* piety, or mercy
(I Sam. 24: 4ff.; II Sam. 19: 23). On *Phinehas'* and *Elijah's* zeal
see v.26 (also Sir. 45: 23).

our father, for that he was zealous exceedingly, obtained
55 the covenant of an everlasting priesthood. Joshua, for
56 fulfilling the word, became a judge in Israel. Caleb, for
bearing witness in the congregation, obtained land as an
57 heritage. David, for being merciful, inherited the throne
58 of a kingdom for ever and ever. Elijah, for that he was
exceeding zealous for the Law, was taken up into heaven.
59 Hananiah, Azariah and Mishael, believing (in God),
60 were saved from the flame. Daniel, for his innocency,
61 was delivered from the mouth of the lions. And thus con-
sider ye from generation to generation; — all who hope
62 in Him shall want for nothing. And be not afraid of the
words of a sinful man, for his glory shall be dung and
63 worms. To-day he shall be lifted up, and to-morrow he
shall in no wise be found, because he is returned unto
64 his dust, and his thought is perished. And ye, children,
be strong and show yourselves men on behalf of the Law;
65 for therein shall ye obtain glory. And behold Simon your
brother, I know that he is a man of counsels; give ear
66 unto him alway; he shall be a father unto you. And
Judah Maccabaeus, he hath been strong and mighty
from his youth; he shall be your captain and shall fight
67 the battle of the people. And ye, take you unto you all
those who observe the Law, and avenge the wrong of
68 your people. Render a compensation to the Gentiles, and
take heed to the commandments of the Law.'
69 And he blessed them and was gathered unto his fathers.
70 And he died in the one hundred and forty-sixth year;

[59f.] The story of *Daniel* (v.60) and his three companions
(v.59) is told in Dan. 3 and 6.

[70] *146* S.E. = 166 B.C.E.

[1] The words *who was called* spoil the meter. They are missing
in the Syriac version.

The author pays tribute to Judah by introducing the story of

and his sons buried him in the sepulchres of his fathers
at Modin; and all Israel made great lamentation for
him.

Judah's Initial Progress

And his son Judah, who was called Maccabaeus, rose up   1
    in his stead.
And all his brethren helped him,
And all they that clave unto his father,   2
And they fought with gladness the battle of Israel.

And he extended the glory of his people,   3
And put on a breastplate as a giant,
And girt on his weapons of war.

He set battles in array,
He protected the army with the sword.
And he was like a lion in his deeds: 4

And as a lion's whelp roaring for prey
He pursued the lawless, seeking them out,   5
And burnt up those that troubled his people.

And the lawless lost heart for fear of him,   6
And all the workers of lawlessness were sore troubled;
And deliverance prospered in his hand.

And he angered many kings,   7
And made Jacob glad with his acts.
And his memorial is blessed for ever.

his exploits in a poetical form. Judah is the central figure in the
remarkable events which follow. In the eyes of the people his
personal qualities and extraordinary success made him the incar-
nation of all national ideals.

[5] *burnt up:* a biblical phrase for "destroyed" (unless reference to 5:35, 44; II Macc. 8:33).

⁸ And he went about among the cities of Judah,
   And destroyed the ungodly thereout,
   And turned away wrath from Israel.

⁹ And he was renowned unto the utmost part of the earth,
   And gathered together those who were perishing.

¹⁰ And Apollonius gathered the Gentiles together, and a
¹¹ great host from Samaria, to fight against Israel. And
   Judah perceived it, and went forth to meet him, and
   smote him, and slew him; and many fell wounded to
¹² death, and the rest fled. And they took their spoils; and
   Judah took the sword of Apollonius, and therewith
   fought he all his days.
¹³ And Seron, the commander of the host of Syria, heard
   that Judah had gathered a gathering and a congregation
   of faithful men with him, and of such as went out to
¹⁴ war; and he said: 'I will make a name for myself, and
   get me glory in the kingdom; and I will fight against
   Judah and them that are with him, that set at nought the
¹⁵ word of the king.' And he went up again; and there went
   up with him a mighty army of the ungodly to help him,
¹⁶ to take vengeance on the children of Israel. And he came
   near to the ascent of Bethhoron; and Judah went forth

[8] By reason of the haughtiness of the foreign invader, who
does not perceive that he is a mere instrument in God's hand,
and by Israel's active repentance, all transgressions are expiated
and Judah is able to turn away the *wrath from Israel*. See II
Macc. 6:12ff. Our author uses the theological interpretation of
history so sparingly that the reconstruction of his spiritual out-
look must remain guesswork.

[10] Apollonius, the "chief collector" of 1:29 (see II Macc.
5:24), raised part of his army among the Samaritans, foes of the
Judeans from the time of the building of the Second Temple.

[12] *the sword of Apollonius.* The use of the battle-honored
sword of the defeated foe, which was frequently superior, is re-

to meet him with a small company. But when they saw [17]
the army coming to meet them, they said unto Judah:
'What? shall we be able, being a small company, to fight
against so great and strong a multitude? And we, for our
part, are faint, having tasted no food this day.' And Ju- [18]
dah said: 'It is an easy thing for many to be shut up in
the hands of a few, and there is no difference in the sight
of Heaven to save by many or by few; for victory in bat- [19]
tle standeth not in the multitude of an host, but strength
is from Heaven. They come unto us in fulness of inso- [20]
lence and lawlessness, to destroy us and our wives and
our children, for to spoil us; but we fight for our lives [21]
and our laws. And He Himself will discomfit them be- [22]
fore our face; but as for you, be ye not afraid of them.'
Now when he had left off speaking, he leapt suddenly [23]
upon them, and Seron and his army were discomfited before him. And they pursued them at the descent of Beth- [24]
horon unto the plain; and there fell of them about eight
hundred men; and the rest fled into the land of the Philistines.

Then began the fear of Judah and of his brethren, and [25]
the dread fell upon the nations round about them. And [26]
his name came near even unto the king; and every nation told of the battles of Judah.

ported of many heroes of antiquity (e.g., David, I Sam. 21:9).

[13] *a gathering and a congregation.* Judah's ill-armed first adherents did not give the impression of a regular army.

[16] *Bethhoron,* or Bet Horon, was the key to Jerusalem, domi-
nating the ascent from the coastal plain to the hills.

[18ff.] Judah's speech before the battle is most effective, his
thought of wives and children moving, his conviction of the justice of the cause genuine. Modern war appeals use similar ideas.
The contrast between the multitude and the few became a classic,
and is impressively represented in the Hanukkah prayers as well
as in Handel's oratorio Judas Maccabaeus.

The First Major Successes

27 But when Antiochus the king heard these words he was full of indignation; and he sent and gathered together all the forces of his kingdom, an exceeding strong army.

28 And he opened his treasury and gave his forces pay for a year, and commanded them to be ready for every need.

29 And he saw that the money failed from his treasures, and that the tributes of the country were small, because of the dissension and harm which he had brought upon the land in seeking to take away the laws which had been

30 from the earliest times; and he feared that he would not have enough, as at other times, for the charges and the gifts which he gave aforetime with a liberal hand, — and he was more lavish than the kings that were before

31 him. He was exceedingly perplexed in his mind; so he determined to go to Persia, and to take tributes of the

32 countries, and to gather much money. And he left Lysias, an honourable man, and one of the seed royal, over the affairs of the king from the river Euphrates unto the bor-

33 ders of Egypt, and to bring up his son Antiochus until

34 he should return. And he delivered unto him the half of the forces and the elephants, and gave him charge over all the things that he would have done and concerning

[28] Antiochus employed a mercenary army. Its morale depended on regular pay. The Jewish fighters, however, were volunteer patriots.

[30] Ancient writers mention the king's disproportionate gifts and love for expensive public displays. He somewhat resembles Nero.

[31] The king tried to continue his policy of temple robbery in the East, only to encounter similar opposition.

[34] *elephants* played an important role in ancient warfare. Very much like modern tanks, they crushed obstacles in their

them that dwell in Judaea and Jerusalem that he should 35
send a host against them to root out and destroy the
strength of Israel and the remnant of Jerusalem, and to
take away their memorial from the place; and that he 36
should make strangers to dwell in all their borders, and
that he should divide their land by lot. And the king took 37
the half that remained of the forces, and removed from
Antioch, from his royal city, in the one hundred and
forty-seventh year; and he passed over the river Euphrates, and went through the upper countries.

And Lysias chose Ptolemy the son of Dorymenes, and 38
Nicanor, and Gorgias, mighty men of the king's friends;
and with them he sent forty thousand footmen, and 39
seven thousand horse, to go into the land of Judah, and
destroy it, according to the king's command. And they 40
removed with all their host, and came and pitched near
Emmaus in the plain country. And the merchants of the 41
country heard tell of them, and took silver and gold exceeding much, together with fetters, and came into the
camp, to take the children of Israel as slaves. And there
were added unto them troops from Syria and from the
land of the Philistines.

And Judah and his brethren saw that evils were multi- 42
plied, and that the forces of the enemy were encamping

way, were difficult to attack, permitted observation of the battle-
field, carried troops, and were a demoralizing factor. Syria's use
of elephants violated the Roman armistice terms of 190.

[37] *Antioch:* in Syria, on the Orontes. *147* S.E. = 166/165 B.C.E.

[40] *Emmaus,* today Amwas, where plain and hills meet, twenty
miles from Jerusalem on the road to Jaffa.

[41] *as slaves.* The slave market was of vital importance for ancient economy which was built on slavery. Apart from the in-
debted or unemployed who were forced to sell themselves or their
children, prisoners of war were the main source of supply.

in their borders; and they took knowledge of the king's
commands which he had put forth to bring about the
43 destruction and annihilation of the people. So they said,
each man to his neighbour: 'Let us raise up the ruin of
our people, and let us fight for our people and the Holy
44 Place.' And the congregation was gathered together, so
as to be ready for battle, and to pray and to ask for
mercy and compassion.

45 And Jerusalem was uninhabited like a wilderness,
There was none of her offspring that went in or went out.
And the Sanctuary was trodden down,
And the sons of strangers (dwelt) in the citadel,
A lodging place for Gentiles;
And joy was taken away from Jacob,
And the pipe and the harp ceased.

46 And they gathered themselves together, and came to
Mizpeh, over against Jerusalem; for in Mizpeh there
47 had been aforetime a place of prayer for Israel. And
they fasted that day, and put on sackcloth, and put ashes
48 upon their heads, and rent their clothes. And they spread
out the roll of the Law, (one of those) concerning which
the Gentiles were wont to make search in order to depict
49 upon them likenesses of their idols. And they brought
the priestly garments, and the firstfruits, and the tithes;
and they shaved the Nazirites who had accomplished
50 their days. And they cried aloud toward heaven, saying:

[46] Once, Samuel had blessed a similar gathering at *Mizpeh*,
close to Jerusalem (I Sam. 7:6).

[48] *they spread out the roll*, to demonstrate how far the fury
of pagan sacrilege had gone. — It seems that according to the
original Hebrew text of this verse, which is mistranslated in the
Greek, the scroll was opened and the passage chanced upon used
as an oracle or battle cry (see II Macc. 8:23).

[49] *priestly garments, the firstfruits, the tithes* and the sacrifice
terminating the *Nazirites'* vow of abstinence, of course, had their

'What shall we do with these men, and whither shall we carry them away? For thy Holy Place is trodden down [51] and defiled, and thy priests are in heaviness and brought low. And, behold, the Gentiles are gathered together [52] to destroy us; thou knowest what things they imagine against us. How shall we be able to stand before them [53] unless thou help us?' And they sounded with the trum- [54] pets, and cried with a loud voice.

And after this Judah appointed leaders of the people, [55] captains of thousands, and captains of hundreds, and captains of fifties, and captains of tens. And he said to [56] them that were building houses, and were betrothing wives, and were planting vineyards, and were fearful, that they should return, each man to his own house, according to the Law. And the army removed, and en- [57] camped on the south of Emmaus. And Judah said: 'Gird [58] yourselves, and be valiant men; and be ready on the morrow to fight against these Gentiles that are assembled together against us to destroy us, and our Holy Place; for it is better for us to die in battle than to look [59] upon the evils that have come upon our nation and the Holy Place. Nevertheless, as may be the will in heaven, [60] so shall he do.'

And Gorgias took five thousand men, and a thousand [1] chosen horse; and the army moved by night so that it [2]

place in the Jerusalem Temple. Their display at Mizpeh was to publicize the great dimension of the national calamity.

[55] *appointed leaders:* the first permanent military organization of the people's army.

[56] *they should return,* in accordance with Deut. 20: 5–8, a measure applied in order to strengthen the morale of army and home-front.

[1] *the army.* Reference is to the special force under Gorgias.

[2] *men of the citadel:* Jewish Hellenists from the Acra.

might fall upon the Jews and smite them suddenly; and
3 men from the citadel were his guides. And Judah heard
thereof, and he removed, he and the valiant men, that
he might smite the king's host, which was at Emmaus,
4 while as yet the forces were dispersed from the camp.
5 And Gorgias came into the camp of Judah by night, and
found no man; and he sought them in the mountains,
6 for he said: 'These men flee from us.' And as soon it was
day, Judah appeared in the plain with three thousand
men; howbeit, they had not armour nor swords as they
7 would have wished. And they saw the camp of the Gentiles strong and fortified, and horsemen compassing it
8 round about; and these were experienced in war. And
Judah said to the men that were with him: 'Fear ye not
9 their multitude, neither be ye afraid of their onset. Remember how our fathers were saved in the Red Sea,
10 when Pharaoh pursued them with a host. And now, let
us cry unto heaven, if he will have mercy upon us, and
will remember the covenant of the fathers, and destroy
11 this army before our face to-day; and all the Gentiles
will know that there is one who redeemeth and saveth
12 Israel.' And the strangers lifted up their eyes and saw
13 them coming against them, and they went out of the
14 camp to battle. And they that were with Judah sounded

[8] *fear ye not their multitude.* At all times, small armies have
been able to rout large contingents. In a more complete version
of this speech in II Macc. 8:19f., Judah cites two examples from
Jewish history.

[13] *went . . . to battle:* the Syrians were taken by surprise and
unable to make proper preparations (Josephus).

[14] *discomfited:* defeated in battle.

[15] *Gazera* is the biblical Gezer, *Azotus,* Ashdod, *Jamnia* the
renowned Yavneh (Jabneh), later the seat of Yohanan ben Zak-
kai's academy, all in *the plain* of Judea (according to two Greek

the trumpets, and joined battle, and the Gentiles were
discomfited, and fled unto the plain. And all the hind- [15]
most fell by the sword; and they pursued them unto
Gazera, and unto the plains of Idumaea and Azotus
and Jamnia; and there fell of them about three thousand
men.

And Judah and his host returned from pursuing after [16]
them; and he said unto the people: 'Be not greedy of the [17]
spoils, for a battle is before us, and Gorgias and his host [18]
are nigh unto us in the mountain. But stand ye now
against our enemies, and fight them, and afterwards take
the spoils with boldness.' While Judah was yet saying [19]
these things, there appeared a part of them peering out
from the mountain; and they saw that (their host) had [20]
been put to flight, and that (the Jews) were burning the
camp, — for the smoke that was seen made manifest
what had been done. And when they perceived these [21]
things they were sore afraid; and perceiving also the
army of Judah in the plain ready for battle, they all fled [22]
into the land of the Philistines. And Judah returned to [23]
the spoil of the camp, and took much gold and silver,
and blue, and sea-purple, and great riches. And as they [24]
returned they sang a song of thanksgiving and blessed
to heaven: 'Good (is the Lord), for his mercy endureth [25]

versions "Judea" instead of *Idumaea,* which was mountainous
and farther away).

[18] *Gorgias and his host:* the main body of the Syrians under
Nicanor and Gorgias.

[22] *the land of the Philistines* (Philistea) was the southern part
of the coastal plain. It gave its name to the whole of "Palestine."

[23] *blue and sea-purple:* precious ancient cloth, frequently
mentioned in the Bible. The purple dye was manufactured from
slimy sea-shells in large factories in Phoenicia.

[24] *Good is the Lord:* freely quoted from the Psalms of thanksgiving (Hallel), which repeat this refrain (Pss. 118:1ff.; 136).

for ever.' And Israel had a great deliverance that day.

26 But as many of the Gentiles as had been saved came
27 and reported to Lysias all that had happened. And when
he heard all he was confounded and discouraged, both
because it had not happened unto Israel as he had
wished, and because the things which the king had commanded him had not come about.
28 And in the next year he gathered together sixty thousand
chosen men, and five thousand horse, to make war upon
29 them. And they came into Judaea, and encamped at
Bethsura, and Judah met them with ten thousand men.
30 And he saw that the army was strong, and he prayed,
and said: 'Blessed art thou, O saviour of Israel, who
didst bring to nought the onslaught of the giant by the
hand of thy servant David, and didst deliver the army
of the Philistines into the hands of Jonathan the son of
31 Saul and of his armour-bearer. Shut up this army in the
hands of thy people Israel, that with their host and their
32 horsemen they may be put to shame. Give them fearful-
ness of heart, and cause the boldness of their strength
to melt away, and let them quake at their destruction.
33 Cast them down with the sword of them that love thee,
and let all that know thy name praise thee with songs of
thanksgiving.'

[29] *Bethsura* (Bet-Zur) "rocky place," the border fortress
eighteen miles south of Jerusalem.

ten thousand: Judah's army grew in proportion to his successes.

[30] The period of the Second Temple was the time of the flour-
ishing of the individual and communal prayer in Israel. The
biblical references are to I Sam. 17:40ff. and 14:1ff.

[34] *five thousand* casualties is a moderate number for a decisive defeat. II Macc. 11:11 has 12,600.

And they joined battle; and there fell of the army of 34
Lysias about five thousand men, and they fell down
over against them. But when Lysias saw that his array 35
had been put to flight, and the boldness that had come
upon them that were with Judah, and how ready they
were either to live or die nobly, he removed to Antioch,
and gathered together mercenary troops, that he might
come again into Judaea with an even greater army.

The Restitution of the Traditional
Worship in Jerusalem

But Judah and his brethren said: 'Behold, our enemies 36
are discomfited; let us go up to cleanse the Holy Place
and re-dedicate it.' And all the army was gathered to- 37
gether, and they went unto mount Zion. And they saw 38
our sanctuary laid desolate, and the altar profaned, and
the gates burned up, and shrubs growing in the courts as
in a forest or upon one of the mountains, and the chambers pulled down; and they rent their garments, and 39
made great lamentation, and put ashes on their heads;
and they fell on their faces to the ground, and they blew 40
the solemn blasts upon the trumpets, and cried unto
heaven. Then Judah appointed men to fight against 41
those in the citadel, until he should have cleansed the

[37] a celebration of victory and the punishment of the traitors
preceded the rededication.

[38] *the gates burned up:* the separating walls of the inner
courts had been torn down to make the Temple a pagan sanctuary. The *shrubs* may have been one of the newly planted sacred
groves of paganism.

[42] *blameless priests:* without physical (Josephus, Antiquities
3:12:2) and moral blemish (Ps. 132:9); *who had delight in
the Law:* who had not joined the Greek party.

⁴² Holy Place. And he chose blameless priests, such as had
⁴³ delight in the Law; and they cleansed the Holy Place,
and bare out the stones of defilement into an unclean
⁴⁴ place. And they took counsel concerning the altar of
burnt offerings, which had been profaned, what they
⁴⁵ should do with it. And a good idea occurred to them, to
pull it down, lest it should be a reproach unto them, be-
⁴⁶ cause the Gentiles had defiled it; so they pulled down
the altar, and laid down the stones in the mountain of
the House, in a convenient place, until a prophet should
⁴⁷ come and decide concerning them. And they took whole
stones according to the Law, and built a new altar after
⁴⁸ the fashion of the former; and they built the Holy Place,
and the inner parts of the house, and hallowed the
⁴⁹ courts. And they made the holy vessels new, and they
brought the candlestick, and the altar of burnt offerings
⁵⁰ and of incense, and the table, into the temple. And they
burned incense upon the altar, and they lighted the
lamps that were upon the candlestick in order to give
⁵¹ light in the temple. And they set loaves upon the table,
and hung up the veils, and finished all the works which

[43] *the stones of defilement,* from the Zeus altar on top of the
altar of burnt-offerings. The latter, although hallowed by ancient
usage, was now desecrated through idol worship.

[46] *until a prophet should come and decide.* In all matters concerning institutions of the early Second Commonwealth, which
had been founded by the last prophets (Ezra, Nehemiah, Hag-
gai, Zechariah and Malachi), only an authority of the same rank
could sanction changes (see 9:27; 14:41). — It is difficult to
determine whether the author expects more prophets to come
(see Deut. 18:18) or believes that prophecy had ceased and
would be renewed with the return of Elijah in the messianic age.

[47] *according to the Law,* i.e. Exod. 20:25, Deut. 27:5f., no
iron could be used in cutting the stones, iron being considered a
profane and warlike element in early Israel.

they had undertaken. And they rose up early in the [52] morning on the twenty-fifth of the ninth month, which is the month Kislev, in the one hundred and forty-eighth year, and offered sacrifice, according to the Law, [53] upon the new altar of burnt offerings which they had made. At the corresponding time and on the correspond- [54] ing day on which the Gentiles had profaned it, on that day was it dedicated afresh, with songs and harps and lutes, and with cymbals. And all the people fell upon [55] their faces, and worshipped and gave praise unto heaven, to Him who had prospered them. And they celebrated [56] the dedication of the altar for eight days, and offered burnt offerings with gladness, and sacrificed a sacrifice of deliverance and praise. And they decked the forefront [57] of the temple with crowns of gold and small shields, and dedicated afresh the gates and the chambers, and furnished them with doors. And there was exceeding great [58] gladness among the people, and the reproach of the Gentiles was turned away. And Judah and his brethren and [59] the whole congregation of Israel ordained, that the days of the dedication of the altar should be kept in their sea-

[51] *loaves:* the twelve cakes of Lev. 24: 5ff. — *Veils* separated the Holy of Holies from a sacred anteroom, and the latter from the outer court.

[52] *early:* in time for the morning sacrifice. — *148* S.E. = 163 B.C.E.

[56] This first celebration of Hanukkah resembled the Feast of Tabernacles (Sukkot), which also lasted *eight days* and had not been observed that year owing to the war (II Macc. 1:9; 10:6f.).

[57] The *crowns* and *shields* were decorations such as used by Solomon (I Kings 10:17) and the Jews of Alexandria (Philo).

[59] "Hanukkah" or the "Feast of Lights," as this festival became known, was possibly meant to counter the influence of the

sons year by year for eight days, from the twenty-fifth
60 of the month Kislev, with gladness and joy. And at that
season they built high walls and strong towers around
mount Zion, lest haply the Gentiles should come and
61 tread them down, as they had done aforetime. And he
set there a force to keep it, and they fortified Bethsura
to keep it, that the people might have a stronghold over
against Idumaea.

Violent Pagan Reaction and
Maccabaean Countermeasures

1 And it came to pass, when the Gentiles round about
heard that the altar had been built and the sanctuary
dedicated, as aforetime, that they were exceeding wroth.
2 And they determined to destroy the race of Jacob that
were in the midst of them, and they began to slay and to
3 destroy among the people. And Judah fought against
the children of Esau in Idumaea at Akrabattine, because
they annoyed Israel by their attacks; and he smote them
with a great slaughter, and humbled them, and took
4 spoils from them. And he remembered the malice of the

pagan winter-solstice feast, apart from recalling the day of profa-
nation (v.54). For the pious the lights became a symbol of the
victory of the Law, or in accordance with a later legend, of the
miraculous power of a tiny cruse of sacred oil, and the pagan
significance of the date was forgotten.

[3] *the children of Esau* or Edom, Jacob's brother: the Edo-
mites or Idumeans (Gen. 36), the southern neighbors of the
Jews.

Akrabattine, from the Heb. "ascent of scorpions," a spot southwest of the Dead Sea.

[4] *Baean* was an Idumean tribe or town.

[5] *towers:* part of the defense system of the towns or the fortified watchtowers and silos in the fields, which were characteris-

children of Baean, who were unto the people a snare and a stumbling-block, lying in wait for them in the ways. And they were shut up by him in the towers; and he en-⁵ camped against them, and utterly destroyed them, and burned with fire the towers of the place, with all that were therein. Then he passed over to the children of ⁶ Ammon, and found a mighty band, and much people, and Timotheus their leader. And he fought many bat-⁷ tles with them, and they were discomfited before him, and he smote them; and he gat possession of Jazer and ⁸ the villages thereof, and returned again into Judaea.

And the Gentiles that were in Gilead gathered them-⁹ selves together against the Israelites that were on their borders, to destroy them; and they fled unto the strong-hold of Dathema. And they sent letters unto Judah and ¹⁰ his brethren, saying: 'The Gentiles that are round about us are gathered together against us to destroy us; and ¹¹ they are preparing to come and get possession of the stronghold whereunto we have fled for refuge; and Ti-motheus is leading their host. Now, therefore, come and ¹² deliver us from their hand, for a number of us are fallen,

tic of the ancient Palestinian countryside (Judg. 9:49; II Kings 17:9).

[6] *he passed over,* i.e. to the land east of the Jordan, northeast of the Dead Sea. — The Greek name of the Ammonite leader shows how far Hellenism had spread.

[8] *Jazer,* a town east of the Jordan, successively Amorite, Jewish, Ammonite (Josh. 13:25). *gat possession* indicates a temporary occupation but not permanent annexation.

[9] These pagans formed a confederacy (see v.38) and endangered the survival of the entire Jewish diaspora in *Gilead* (Transjordan between the rivers Arnon and Yarmuk). The fortress of *Dathema* may be identical with Charax (El-Kerak, II Macc. 12:17).

¹³ and all our brethren that were in the parts of Tubias
have been put to death, and they have carried into cap-
tivity their wives and their children and their belongings, and have destroyed there about a thousand men.'
¹⁴ While the letters were yet being read, behold, there came
other messengers from Galilee with their garments rent,
¹⁵ bringing a report to the following effect, saying: 'There
be gathered together against them men from Ptolemais,
and Tyre and Sidon, and all Galilee of the Gentiles, to
¹⁶ consume us.' Now when Judah and the people heard
these words, there assembled together a great gathering to consult what they should do for their brethren
who were in tribulation and being attacked by the en-
¹⁷ emy. And Judah said unto Simon his brother: 'Choose
out men for thyself, and go and deliver thy brethren in
Galilee, while I and Jonathan my brother will go into
¹⁸ Gilead.' And he left Joseph the son of Zacharias, and
Azarias, as leaders of the people, with the rest of the
¹⁹ army, in Judaea, to guard it. And he commanded them,
saying: 'Take ye the charge of this people, and engage
²⁰ not in battle with the Gentiles until we return.' And
three thousand men were allotted unto Simon to go into
Galilee, and eight thousand men unto Judah to go into
Gilead.
²¹ And Simon went into Galilee, and engaged in many battles with the Gentiles, and the Gentiles were discom-

[13] *Tubias* or the "Land of Tob" (Judg. 11:3): southeast of
the Sea of Galilee.

[15] *Ptolemais* (Accho, Akka, Acre), *Tyre* and *Sidon* are Phoenician seaports. *Galilee of the Gentiles* was Upper Galilee with its
mixed pagan population.

[23] *Arbatta* is the lower Jordan valley, unless error for Nar-
batha, west of Samaria.

[25] *the Nabataeans* (Nebaioth, Gen. 25:13) were an important

fited before him. And he pursued them unto the gate of [22]
Ptolemais; and there fell of the Gentiles about three
thousand men, and he took their spoils. And he took [23]
those that were in Galilee and Arbatta with their wives
and children, and brought them into Judaea with great
gladness.

And Judah Maccabaeus and his brother Jonathan passed [24]
over Jordan, and went three days' journey in the wilderness; and they fell in with the Nabataeans, and these met [25]
them in a peaceful manner, and recounted to them all
things that had befallen their brethren in Gilead; and [26]
how that many of them were shut up in Bosora, and Bosor, and Alema, Casphor, Maked, and Carnaim, — all
these cities strong and great; and how that they were [27]
shut up in the rest of the cities of Gilead, and that on the
morrow (the enemies) had planned to encamp against
the stronghold and to take it, and to destroy all those
who were in it in one day. And Judah and his army [28]
turned suddenly by the way of the wilderness unto Bosora; and he took the city, and slew all the males with
the edge of the sword, and took all their spoils, and
burned it with fire. And he removed thence by night, and [29]
went on until he reached the stronghold. And when it [30]
was morning they lifted up their eyes, and behold, a
great multitude which could not be numbered, bearing
ladders and engines of war, to take the stronghold; and

Hellenized Arab tribe. Their capital was Petra. They were gradually becoming engaged in commerce.

[26] *Bosora:* Bozrah in Moab; *Bosor* (Bezer), *Alema, Casphor,*
Maked, and *Carnaim* (Deut. 1 : 4) : cities of Gilead.

[27] *shut up:* the Jewish settlers were kept prisoners.
   the stronghold: Dathema (v.9).

[30] Among the ancient *engines of war* were catapults and bat-
tering-rams, the latter mounted on mobile siege-towers.

they were fighting against them (that were in the strong-
[31] hold). And when Judah saw that the battle had begun,
and that the cry of the city went up to heaven, with
[32] trumpets and a great sound, he said unto the men of his
[33] host: 'Fight this day for your brethren.' And he went
forth behind them in three companies, and they sounded
[34] with trumpets, and cried out in prayer. And the army
of Timotheus perceived that it was Maccabaeus, and
they fled from before him; and he smote them with a
great slaughter; and there fell of them on that day about
[35] eight thousand men. And he turned aside to Mizpeh and
fought against it, and took it, and slew all the males
thereof, and took the spoils thereof, and burned it with
[36] fire. From thence he removed, and took Casphor, Maked, Bosor, and the other cities of Gilead.
[37] Now after these things Timotheus gathered another
army, and encamped over against Raphon, beyond the
[38] brook. And Judah sent men to espy the army; and they
reported to him, saying: 'All the Gentiles that are round
about us are gathered together unto them, an exceeding
[39] great host; and they have hired Arabians to help them,
and are encamping beyond the brook, ready to come
[40] against thee to battle.' And Judah went to meet them.
And Timotheus said unto the captains of his host, when
Judah and his army drew nigh unto the brook of water:
'If he pass over unto us first, we shall not be able to
withstand him, for he will mightily prevail against us;

[35] *Mizpeh:* in Gilead (Judg. 11:29).

[37] *Raphon* was one of the cities of the Decapolis, a province
of Palestine which included ten Greek cities, nine of them in
Transjordan (see v.52).

[40f.] Timotheus speculated that hesitancy on the part of Judah
would demoralize the impetuous Jewish army.

but if he be afraid, and encamp beyond the river, we will [41] cross over unto him, and prevail against him.' Now [42] when Judah came nigh unto the brook of water, he placed the officers of the people by the brook, and commanded them, saying: 'Suffer no men to encamp, but let all come to the battle.' And he crossed over first [43] against them, and all his people after him; and all the Gentiles were discomfited before his face, and cast away their arms, and fled unto the temple of Carnaim. And [44] they took the city, and burned the temple with fire, together with all that were therein. And Carnaim was subdued; neither could they stand any longer before the face of Judah.

And Judah gathered together all Israel, them that were [45] in Gilead, from the least unto the greatest, and their wives, and their children, and their belongings, an exceeding great army, that they might come into the land of Judah. And they came as far as Ephron; and this was [46] a large city at the pass, exceeding strong; it was not possible to turn aside from it either to the right or to the left, but one had to go through the midst of it. And they [47] of the city shut them out, and stopped up the gates with stones. And Judah sent unto them with words of peace, [48] saying: 'We would pass through thy land to go into our own land; and none shall harm you, we will only pass by on our feet.' But they would not open unto him. And [49] Judah commanded proclamation to be made in the

[45] Judah's victories saved the Jews in those parts, but peaceful settlement was still impossible. Evacuation to Judea (see v.23) was the only solution.

[46] *Ephrun* (Gefrun), east of the Jordan.

[48] *pass through.* This request was frequently made to ancient cities situated in mountain passes, and frequently refused (Num. 20:17; 21:22), probably for fear of treacherous conquest.

army, that each man should encamp in the place where
50 he was. And the men of the host encamped; and they
fought against the city all that day and all that night;
51 and the city was delivered unto his hands; and he destroyed all the males with the edge of the sword, and
rased the city, and took the spoils thereof, and passed
52 through the city over them that were slain. And they
went over Jordan into the great plain over against Beth-
53 shan. And Judah gathered together those that lagged behind, and encouraged the people all the way through un-
54 til he came into the land of Judah. And they went up to
mount Zion with gladness and joy, and offered whole
burnt offerings, because not so much as one of them was
slain until they returned in peace.
55 And in the days when Judah and Jonathan were in the
land of Gilead, and Simon his brother in Galilee before
56 Ptolemais, Joseph the son of Zacharias, and Azarias,
leaders of the armies, heard of their exploits and of the
57 war, — what things they had done; and they said: 'Let
us also make a name for ourselves, and let us go fight
58 against the Gentiles that are round about us. And they
gave charge unto the men of the host that was with them,
59 and went toward Jamnia. And Gorgias and his men came
60 out of the city to meet them in battle. And Joseph and
Azarias were put to flight, and were pursued unto the
borders of Judaea; and there fell on that day of the

[52] *the great plain* extended west from the biblical *Bethshan*
(today Beisan, west of the Jordan), which under the name of
Scythopolis was at that time one of the ten cities of the Decapolis (see v.37).

[54] The complete absence of losses was true only for the retreat
after the battle of Bethshan.

[63] *the man Judah:* as so many phrases in this book, a literal
translation from the Hebrew.

people of Israel about two thousand men. And there was [61]
a great overthrow among the people, because they heark-
ened not unto Judah and his brethren, thinking to do
some exploit. But they were not of the seed of those men, [62]
by whose hand deliverance was given unto Israel. But [63]
the man Judah and his brethren were glorified exceedingly in the sight of all Israel, and of all the Gentiles,
wheresoever their name was heard of; and men gathered [64]
unto them, acclaiming.

And Judah and his brethren went forth, and fought [65]
against the children of Esau in the land toward the south;
and he smote Hebron and the villages thereof, and
pulled down the strongholds thereof, and burned the
towers thereof round about. And he removed to go into [66]
the land of the Philistines, and he went through Marisa.
In that day priests fell in battle, desiring themselves to [67]
do exploits, in that they went out to the war unadvisedly.
And Judah turned aside to Azotus, to the land of the [68]
Philistines, and pulled down their altars, and burned the
carved images of their gods and took the spoil of their
cities, and returned into the land of Judah.

[64] *men gathered unto him.* The number of Jewish volunteers
was ever increasing. Also, pagan merchants followed the army.

[65] *Hebron,* twenty miles south of Jerusalem, had been Jewish
territory in the First Commonwealth.

[66] *Marisa:* Maresha, in the plain of Judea.

[67] According to II Macc. 12:38ff., the death of the priests
was a punishment for their taking pagan amulets from the temples of Jamnia.

[68] *Azotus:* see 4:15.

Death of Antiochus

1 And king Antiochus was journeying through the upper
countries; and he heard that Elymais, in Persia, was a
2 city renowned for riches, for silver and gold, and that
the temple which was in it was rich exceedingly, and that
therein were golden shields, and breastplates, and arms,
which Alexander, son of Philip, the Macedonian king,
who reigned first among the Greeks, had left behind
3 there. So he came and sought to take the city, and to
pillage it; but he was not able to do so because the thing
4 had become known to them of the city. And they rose up
against him to battle; and he fled, and removed thence
with great heaviness, to return to Babylon.
5 And there came one bringing him tidings into Persia
that the armies, which went against the land of Judah,
6 had been put to flight; and that Lysias had gone forth
at the head of a strong army, and had been put to shame
before them; and that they had waxed strong by reason
of arms and power, and with store of spoils, which they
7 took from the armies that they had cut off; and that they
had pulled down the abomination which he had built
upon the altar that was in Jerusalem; and that they had

[2] The wealth of ancient temples was constituted by (1) sacrificial gifts, (2) national trophies on display, (3) money and valu-
ables deposited for safekeeping.

[4] *they rose up.* This shows that the pillage of Jerusalem and
the Judean uprising were not unique.

[10] The last words of the king are hardly authentic but repre-
sent what a contemporary Jew expected him to say.

[12] *I remember the evils.* Sentimentality before his end would
fit the descriptions of Antiochus' character, but his confession
could not have had Jerusalem as its sole theme. The priests of

compassed about the sanctuary with high walls, as formerly, and Bethsura, his city. And it came to pass when 8 the king heard these words, he was struck with amazement and greatly moved; and he laid him down upon his bed, and fell sick for grief, because it had not befallen him as he had looked for. And he was there many 9 days, because great grief was renewed upon him; and he reckoned that he was about to die. And he called for 10 all his Friends, and said unto them: 'Sleep departeth from mine eyes, and my heart faileth for care. And I said 11 in my heart, Unto what tribulation am I come and how great a flood is it wherein I now am! For I was gracious 12 and beloved in my power. But now I remember the evils which I did at Jerusalem, and that I took all the vessels of silver and gold that were therein, and sent forth to destroy the inhabitants of Judah without a cause. I per- 13 ceive that on this account these evils are come upon me, and behold, I perish through great grief in a strange land.' And he called for Philip, one of his Friends, and 14 set him over all his kingdom, and gave him his diadem, 15 and his robe, and signet-ring, to the end that he should educate Antiochus, his son, and bring him up to be king. And king Antiochus died there in the one hundred and 16 forty-ninth year. And when Lysias knew that the king 17

two other looted temples of Syria asserted that their goddesses (Naneia and Atargatis) had been responsible for Antiochus' punishment.

[14] Lysias seems to have fallen into disfavor owing to his Judean defeats.

[16] *149* s.e. = 163 b.c.e. — In spite of II Macc. 9, according to which Antiochus died of physical causes, the tradition of I Macc., which has him die of insanity, seems to be reliable, since it is found in various forms (grief, hallucinations, raving) in Daniel, and with Polybios and Chrysostom.

[17] *Antiochus* V *Eupator:* "from a noble father."

was dead, he set up Antiochus his son to reign, whom he
had nourished up while yet young, and he called his
name Eupator.

Reverses and Compromises

¹⁸ And they that were in the citadel kept enclosing Israel
round about the sanctuary, and continually sought their
¹⁹ hurt, and acted as a support to the Gentiles. And Judah
purposed to destroy them, and called all the people to-
²⁰ gether to besiege them. And they were gathered together,
and besieged them in the one hundred and fiftieth year;
and he constructed siege-towers against them, and en-
²¹ gines of war. And there came forth some of them that
were shut up, and unto them were joined certain ungodly
²² men of Israel. And they went unto the king and said:
'How long wilt thou not execute judgement and avenge
²³ our brethren? We were willing to serve thy father, and
to walk after his words, and to follow his command-
²⁴ ments. For this cause the children of our people besieged
the citadel, and were alienated from us, and as many of
us as they could light on they killed, and they spoiled
²⁵ our inheritances. And not against us only did they
stretch out their hand, but also against all their border-
²⁶ lands. And, behold, they are encamped this day against
the citadel in Jerusalem with the object of capturing it,
²⁷ and they have fortified the sanctuary and Bethsura. And
if thou art not beforehand with them quickly they will
do greater things than these, and thou wilt not be able

[30] It is highly probable that these figures are exaggerated.

[32] *Beth-zacharias,* three miles south of Bethlehem.

[34] Before the battle elephants were exposed to the smell of
alcoholic liquids in order to incite their ferocity (see III Macc.
5:1).

to control them.' And the king was angry when he heard [28] this; and he gathered together all his Friends, the leaders of his host, and them that were over the horse. And [29] there came unto him from other kingdoms, and from the isles of the sea, bands of mercenaries. And the number of his forces was a hundred thousand footmen, and [30] twenty thousand horsemen, and thirty-two elephants trained for war. And they went through Idumaea, and [31] encamped against Bethsura, and fought against it many days, and made engines of war; but they (that were besieged) came out and burned them with fire, and fought manfully. And Judah removed from the citadel, and en- [32] camped at Beth-zacharias, over against the king's camp. And the king rose early in the morning, and removed the [33] army in its eagerness along the road to Beth-zacharias; and his forces prepared themselves for the battle, and sounded with trumpets. And they showed the elephants [34] the blood of grapes and mulberries, that they might prepare them for the battle. And they divided the beasts [35] among the phalanxes, and they set by each elephant a thousand men armed with coats of mail, and helmets of brass on their heads; and for each beast were appointed five hundred chosen horsemen. These had previously [36] been wherever a beast was; and whithersoever it went, they went together with it; they did not leave it. And [37] towers of wood were upon them, strong and covered, one upon each beast, girt fast upon them with contrivances; and upon each were thirty-two men, fighting from them, and each beast had its Indians. And the residue of the [38]

[35] *phalanxes*. The Macedonians had introduced the phalanx, i.e. tightly closed rows of lance-carrying soldiers, into ancient warfare.

[38] *Indian*. Because the first elephant drivers had come from India, all members of this profession were called Indians.

horsemen he placed on this side and that side, on either
wing of the army, striking terror while covering the pha-
39 lanxes. Now when the sun shone upon the shields of gold
and brass, the mountains shone therewith, and blazed
40 like torches of fire. And a part of the king's army was
spread upon the high mountains, and some on the low
41 ground, and they went on safely and in order. And all
that heard the noise of their multitude, and of the march-
ing of the multitude, and the rattle of the arms, did
quake; for the army was exceeding great and strong.
42 And Judah and his army drew near for battle, and there
fell of the king's army six hundred men.
43 And Eleazar Avaran saw one of the beasts armed with
royal breastplates, and he was higher than all the other
beasts, so that it appeared as though the king were upon
44 it; and he gave himself to deliver his people and to ac-
45 quire an everlasting name; and he ran upon it coura-
geously into the midst of the phalanx, and slew on the
right hand and on the left, and they parted asunder from
46 him on this side and on that; and he crept under the elephant, and thrust him from beneath, and slew it; and it
47 fell to the earth upon him, and he died there. And when
they saw the strength of the royal army, and the fierce
onslaught of the hosts, they turned away from them.
48 But they of the king's army went up to Jerusalem to
meet them, and the king encamped toward Judaea, and
49 toward mount Zion. And he made peace with those of
Bethsura; for they came out of the city, because they
had no food there to be shut up therein, because it was
50 a sabbath to the land. And the king took Bethsura, and
51 appointed a garrison there to keep it. And he encamped
against the sanctuary many days, and set there siege-

[49] *a Sabbath of the land.* In the sabbatical year the fields were
neither sown nor reaped (Lev. 25:2ff.).

towers, and engines of war, and instruments for casting
fire and stones, and pieces to cast darts and slings. And 52
they who were besieged also made engines against their
engines, and fought for many days. But there were no 53
victuals in the store-chambers because it was the seventh
year, and they that had fled for safety to Judaea from
the Gentiles had eaten up the residue of the store; and 54
there were but a few men left in the sanctuary, because
the famine prevailed against them, and they were scattered, each man to his own place.

And Lysias heard that Philip, whom Antiochus the king 55
— while he was yet alive — appointed to nourish up his
son Antiochus that he might be king, had returned from 56
Persia and Media, and with him the forces that went
with the king, and that he was seeking to take unto him
the government. And he made haste, and gave consent 57
to depart; and he said to the king and to the leaders of
the host and to the men: 'We languish daily, and our
food is scant, and the place which we are besieging is
strong, and the affairs of the kingdom lie upon us; now 58
therefore let us give the right hand to these men, and
make peace with them, and with all their nation; and 59
let us settle with them that they be permitted to walk
after their own laws, as aforetime; for because of their
laws which we abolished were they angered, and did all
these things.' And the saying pleased the king and the 60
leaders, and he sent unto them to make peace; and they
accepted thereof. And the king and the leaders sware 61
unto them in accordance with these conditions; thereupon they came forth from the stronghold, and the king
entered into mount Zion. But when he saw the strength 62

[58] *the right hand:* the symbol of reconciliation. The peace
treaty granted religious freedom to the Jews, who in turn recog-

of the place, he set at nought the oath which he had
sworn, and gave commandment to pull down the wall
63 round about. And he removed in haste, and returned
unto Antioch, and found Philip master of the city; and
he fought against him, and took the city by force.

Another Maccabaean War

1 In the one hundred and fifty-first year Demetrius the
son of Seleucus came forth from Rome, and went up
with a few men unto a city by the sea, and reigned there.
2 And it came to pass, when he had formed the purpose
of entering into the house of the kingdom of his fathers,
that the soldiery laid hands on Antiochus and Lysias,
3 to bring them unto him. And when the thing was made
4 known to him, he said: 'Show me not their faces.' And
the soldiery slew them. And Demetrius sat upon the
5 throne of his kingdom. And there came unto him all the
lawless and ungodly men of Israel; and Alcimus led
6 them, desiring to be high-priest. And they accused the
people unto the king, saying: 'Judah and his brethren
have destroyed all thy Friends, and have scattered us
7 from our land. Now therefore send a man whom thou
trustest, and let him go and see all the havock which he
hath made of us and of the king's country, and let him
8 punish them and all that helped them.' And the king
chose Bacchides, of the king's friends, who was ruler in

nized the king as their sovereign. The Maccabees remained "un-
authorized" partisan leaders.

[1] *155* S.E. = 162/161 B.C.E.
Demetrius I Soter ("redeemer") reigned 162–150. He had
lived as a hostage in Rome in place of his uncle Antiochus Epiphanes.

[3] *Show me not their faces:* a hint that he wanted their execu-
tion without actually giving orders for it.

the country beyond the river, and was a great man in
the kingdom, and faithful to the king. And he sent him   9
and the ungodly Alcimus, and made sure to him the
priesthood; and he commanded him to take vengeance
upon the children of Israel.

And they removed, and came with a great host into the   10
land of Judah; and he sent messengers to Judah and his
brethren with words of peace, deceitfully. But they gave   11
no heed to their words; for they saw that they were
come with a great host. And there was gathered together   12
unto Alcimus and Bacchides a company of scribes, to
seek for justice. And the Hasidim were the first among   13
the children of Israel that sought peace of them; for they   14
said: 'One that is a priest of the seed of Aaron is come
with the forces, and he will do us no wrong.' And he spake   15
with them words of peace, and sware unto them, saying:
'We will seek the hurt neither of you nor of your friends.'
And they believed him; and he laid hands on threescore   16
men of them, and he slew them in one day, according to
the words:

> The flesh of thy saints and their blood   17
> They poured out around Jerusalem;
> And there was no man to bury them.

And the fear and the dread of them fell upon all the   18
people, for they said: 'There is neither truth nor judgement in them; for they have broken the covenant and the

[5] *Alcimus* is a Grecized form of the Heb. Eliakim. Being an
ordinary Aaronite, he was, in spite of a previous Syrian appoint-
ment, not eligible for the office of high priest. See 10: 20.

[12] The *scribes* were the legal experts and religious leaders of
the people, backed by the Hasidim.

[16] These victims were former sympathizers of Judah.

[17] This elegy is a condensation of Ps. 79: 2f.

¹⁹ oath which they sware.' And Bacchides removed from
Jerusalem, and encamped in Bezeth; and he sent and
took many of the deserters that were with him, and certain of the people, and slew them, and cast them into
²⁰ the great pit. And he delivered the land to Alcimus, and
left with him a force to aid him; and Bacchides went
away unto the king.

²¹'²² And Alcimus strove for the high-priesthood. And there
were gathered unto him all they that troubled their people, and they got the mastery of the land of Judah, and
²³ did great hurt in Israel. And Judah saw all the mischief
that Alcimus and his company had wrought among the
²⁴ children of Israel, worse than that of the Gentiles; and
he went out into all the coasts of Judaea round about,
and took vengeance on the men that had deserted from
him, and they were restrained from going forth into the
²⁵ country. But when Alcimus saw that Judah and his
company waxed strong, and knew that he was not able
to withstand them, he returned to the king, and brought
evil accusations against them.
²⁶ And the king sent Nicanor, one of his honourable
princes, a man that hated Israel and was their enemy,
²⁷ and commanded him to destroy the people. And Nicanor
came to Jerusalem with a great host; and he sent unto
Judah and his brethren deceitfully with words of peace,
²⁸ saying: 'Let there be no battle between me and you; I

[19] *Bezeth,* "place of olives," today Beit Zeita, south of Beth-
Zacharias, where a "cistern of the heroes" — the great pit? —
is still shown.

[20] After Alcimus' accession to the rule over Judea, Bacchides
saw his task completed, and withdrew.

[24] *they were restrained,* i.e. besieged.

will come with a few men, that I may see your faces in peace.' And he came to Judah, and they saluted one an- 29 other peaceably. But the enemies were ready to take away Judah by violence. And the thing became known 30 to Judah, that he came unto him with deceit; and he was sore afraid of him, and would see his face no more. And 31 when Nicanor knew that his purpose was discovered, he went out to meet Judah in battle beside Capharsalama; and there fell of those with Nicanor about five hundred 32 men, and they fled into the city of David.

And after these things Nicanor went up to mount Zion; 33 and there came some of the priests out of the sanctuary, and some of the elders of the people, to salute him peaceably, and to show him the whole burnt sacrifice that was being offered for the king; but he mocked 34 them, and laughed at them, and polluted them, and spake haughtily, and sware in a rage, saying: 'Unless 35 Judah and his army be now delivered into my hands, it shall be that, if I come again in safety, I will burn up this house.' And he went forth with great wrath. And the 36 priests entered in, and stood before the altar and the temple, and wept and said: 'Thou didst choose this house 37 to be called by thy name, to be a house of prayer and supplication for thy people; take vengeance on this man 38 and his army, and let them fall by the sword; remember their blasphemies, and suffer them not to live any longer.'

[26] This Nicanor, who had been with Demetrius in Rome, is not identical with the one mentioned in 3 : 38.

[29] According to II Macc. 14 : 22, Judah cautiously appeared with troops. According to Josephus he darted back to his body-guard upon Nicanor's giving a suspicious signal to his soldiers.

[33] Prayers and sacrifices were offered for heathen rulers (see

39 And Nicanor went forth from Jerusalem, and encamped
40 in Bethhoron, and there met him the host of Syria. And
Judah encamped in Adasa with three thousand men; and
41 Judah prayed, and said: 'When they that came from the
king blasphemed, thine angel went out and smote among
42 them one hundred and eighty-five thousand. Even so
crush this army before us to-day; and let all the rest
know that he hath spoken wickedly against thy sanctu-
43 ary; and judge him according to his wickedness.' And
the armies joined battle on the thirteenth of the month
Adar; and Nicanor's army was discomfited, and he him-
44 self was the first to fall in the battle. Now when his army
saw that Nicanor was fallen, they cast away their arms,
45 and fled. And they pursued after them a day's journey
from Adasa until thou comest to Gazara, and they
sounded an alarm after them with the solemn trumpets.
46 And they came forth out of all the villages of Judaea
round about, and closed them in; and these turned back
on those behind, and they all fell by the sword, and there
47 was not one of them left. And they took the spoils and
the booty, and they smote off Nicanor's head, and his

Jeremiah's famous advice to the Babylonian exiles, Jer. 29:7
and Ezra 6:10).

[40] *Adasa:* three miles northeast of Bethhoron.

[41] Reference is to an Assyrian onslaught under Sennacherib
(II Kings 18:22ff.).

[43] The difficult terrain, well known to Judeans, enabled their
few men to defeat a large army.
the month Adar usually occurs in March.

[45] the *alarm* was given to call the Judeans in the villages to
arms. The distance between *Adasa* and *Gazara* (4:15) was fifteen miles.

[49] It was a Hellenistic custom to proclaim a new festival after
a victory. "Nicanor Day" remained popular for several centuries
until gradually the Fast of Esther (Esther 4:3) displaced it,

right hand, which he stretched out so haughtily, and
brought them, and hanged them up near Jerusalem. And 48
the people was exceeding glad, and they kept that day
as a day of great gladness. And they ordained that this 49
day should be observed year by year (on) the thirteenth
of Adar. And the land of Judah had rest a little while.   50

The Treaty with the Romans

And Judah heard of the fame of the Romans, that they   1
were valiant men, and that they were friendly disposed
towards all who attached themselves to them, and that
they offered friendship to as many as came unto them,
and that they were valiant men. And they told him about 2
their wars and exploits which they had done among the
Galatians, and how they had conquered them, and
brought them under tribute; and what things they had   3
done in the land of Spain, how they had acquired the
mines of silver and gold there; and how that by their   4
policy and persistence they had conquered the whole
land and the land was exceeding far from them; also of

probably as a result of the rabbinic repudiation of the later
Hasmoneans.

[1ff.] The major conquests of the Romans in the 2nd cent. B.C.E.,
their policy of alliances, and their republican institutions and
puritan ideals made a great impression upon the ancient peoples.
The details of the report, gathered from hearsay, of course, are
not too accurate. The treaty is generally believed to be a historical fact.

offered friendship. Among the allies of Rome were Pergamum
(Asia Minor) and Egypt. In 161 they concluded a similar treaty
with another rebel from the Syrian yoke in Babylonia.

[2] Galatians. The Romans conquered the North Italian Gauls
in 190, and their brothers in Asia Minor in 189 B.C.E.

[3] Vital parts of Spain were acquired after the Second Punic

the kings that had come against them from the uttermost
part of the earth, until they had discomfited them, and
smitten them very sore; and how the rest had given them
5 tribute year by year. Furthermore, of how they had discomfited in battle Philip, and Perseus, king of Chittim,
and them that lifted themselves up against them, and
6 had conquered them; Antiochus also, the great king of
Asia, who had come against them to battle, having a
hundred and twenty elephants, with cavalry, and chariots, and an exceeding great host, — he had also been dis-
7 comfited by them, and they had taken him alive, and
had appointed that both he and such as reigned after him
should give them a great tribute and should give hos-
8 tages, and a 'tract' of land, namely the country of India,
and Media, and Lydia, and of the goodliest of their countries; and how they had taken them from him, and had
9 given them to king Eumenes. Also how they of Greece
10 had purposed to come and destroy them, and the thing
had become known to them, and they had sent against
them a captain, and had fought against them, and many
of them had fallen, wounded to death; and of how they
had made captive their wives and their children, and
had spoiled and conquered their land, and had pulled

War, 208–201, with the Semitic Carthaginians under Hannibal, to
whom v.4 alludes.

[5] *king of Chittim:* read "kings of Chittim." Philip V and Perseus, kings of Macedonia, were defeated in 197 and 168.

[6f.] *Antiochus* III, "the Great," see 1:10. — The *great tribute*
which the Romans imposed on Syria (about $36,000,000) may
have contributed to her oppressive internal financing policies.

[8] Ionia (not *India*), Mysia (not *Media*) and *Lydia* are countries of Asia Minor.

[9] *Eumenes* II, king of Pergamum, 198–158.

[10] Refers to the last desperate effort of the Greeks to retain

down their strongholds, and had brought them into bondage unto this day. And how they had destroyed [11] the residue of the kingdoms and of the isles, as many as had risen up against them, and had made them their servants; but that with their friends and such as re- [12] lied upon them they kept amity; and of how they had conquered the kingdoms that were nigh and those that were far off and that all who heard of their fame were afraid of them. Moreover they told that whom- [13] soever they will to succour and to make kings, become kings; and that whomsoever they will, do they depose; and they are exalted exceedingly; and that for [14] all this none of them did ever put on a diadem, neither did they clothe themselves with purple, to be magnified thereby. They told also how they had made for them- [15] selves a senate house, and how day by day three hundred and twenty men sat in council, consulting alway for the people, to the end that they might be well ordered; and how they committed their government to one [16] man year by year, that he should be over them, and be lord over all their country; and that all are obedient to this one, and that there is neither envy nor emulation among them.

their freedom and the cruel punishment by Rome under the *captain* L. Mummius in 146 (destruction of Corinth, Greece becomes a Roman province). The mention of this event is anachronistic, since Judah had died previously.

[11] The *isles* are Sicily, Sardinia, Corsica, and the Greek archipelago.

[15f.] The Roman Senate never had more than 300 members. Only in emergencies and — in later centuries — in February, did they meet *day by day,* i.e. in permanent session. There were two consuls. Only in times of a national calamity did *one man,* the dictator, rule. These inaccuracies, however, are slight. To a remote spectator who hoped for aid, Rome seemed to be free from inner strife.

¹⁷ And Judah chose Eupolemus, the son of John, the son of Accos, and Jason, the son of Eleazar, and sent them to Rome, to make a league of amity and confederacy with ¹⁸ them, and that they should take the yoke from them, when they saw that the kingdom of the Greeks did keep ¹⁹ Israel in bondage. And they went to Rome, and the way was exceeding long; and they entered into the Senate ²⁰ house, and answered and said: 'Judah, who is also called Maccabaeus, and his brethren, and the whole people of the Jews, have sent us unto you, to make a confederacy and peace with you, and that we might be regis- ²¹ tered your confederates and friends.' And the thing was ²² well-pleasing in their sight. And this is the copy of the writing which they wrote back again on tablets of brass, and sent to Jerusalem, that it might be with them there for a memorial of peace and confederacy:

²³ 'Good success be to the Romans, and to the nations of the Jews, by sea and by land for ever; the sword also ²⁴ and the enemy be far from them. But if war arise for Rome first, or for any of their confederates in all their ²⁵ dominion, the nation of the Jews shall help them as confederates as the occasion shall prescribe to them, with ²⁶ all their heart; and unto them that make war they shall not give neither supply, food, arms, money, or ships, as

[17] *Eupolemos,* the son of a diplomat (II Macc. 4 : 11), and a priest (Accos = Hakkotz, Ezra 2 : 61), was possibly identical with the Hellenistic writer of this name. *Jason* may be the one mentioned in 12 : 16.

[20] *the whole people of the Jews:* an intentional overstatement in order to gain recognition from the Romans, which, in any event, was usually granted to promising revolutionaries.

[23–32] The writer must have known the original document. — According to our translation, the final decision in all vital questions seems to have rested with the Romans, see vv. 25, 27, 28. Other modern translators, however, see complete parity in the

it hath seemed good unto Rome; and they shall observe their obligations, receiving nothing. In the same manner, [27] moreover, if war come first upon the nation of the Jews, the Romans shall help them as confederates with all their soul, as the occasion shall prescribe to them; and [28] to them that are confederates there shall not be given corn, arms, money, or ships, as it hath seemed good unto Rome; and they shall observe these obligations, and that without deceit.' According to these words have the [29] Romans made a treaty with the people of the Jews. But [30] if hereafter the one party or the other shall determine to add or to diminish anything, they shall do it at their pleasure, and whatsoever they shall add or take away shall be established. And as touching the evils which [31] king Demetrius doeth unto you, we have written to him saying: 'Wherefore hast thou made thy yoke heavy upon our friends and confederates the Jews? If, there- [32] fore, they plead any more against thee, we will do them justice, and fight thee by sea and by land.'

Defeat and Death of Judah

And when Demetrius had heard that Nicanor was fallen [1] with his forces in battle, he sent Bacchides and Alcimus

wording of the treaty. — It appears from the Hebraisms that vv. 31f. are a free summary of an appendix to the treaty or an oral communication from the ambassadors.

[26] The mention of *ships* may have been a standard provision in all Roman treaties, or statesmenlike foresight, for the Jews did regain a harbor some years later.

[31] As the next chapter discloses, the Roman pressure on *Demetrius* came too late.

[1ff.] Judah's small but valiant group is defeated before the onslaught of Syria's full military strength, which now is being brought into play.

again into the land of Judah a second time, and the right
2 wing of his army with them. And they went by way of
Gilgal, and encamped against Mesaloth, which is in Arbela, and gat possession of it, and destroyed much peo-
3 ple. And in the first month of the one hundred and fifty-
4 second year they encamped against Jerusalem. And they
removed and went unto Berea, with twenty thousand
5 footmen and two thousand horse. And Judah was encamped at Elasa, and three thousand chosen men with
6 him. And when they saw the multitude of the forces,
that they were many, they feared exceedingly; and
many slipped away from the army; there were not left
7 of them more than eight hundred men. And when Judah
saw that his army slipped away, and that the battle was
imminent for him, he was sore troubled in heart, for that
8 he had no time to gather them together. And he became
desperate, and said to them that were left: 'Let us arise
and go up against our adversaries, if peradventure we
9 may be able to fight against them.' And they turned
from him, saying: 'We shall in no wise be able to withstand them; but let us rather save our lives now; let us
return with our brethren, and fight against them; we are
10 now too few.' Then Judah said: 'Far be it from me to do
this thing, to flee from them! And if our time is come,
let us die manfully for our brethren's sake and not leave

[2] The locations of *Gilgal* — perhaps an error for "Galilee"
(so Josephus) or Gilead (some MSS.) — and *Mesaloth* and
Arbela are unknown.

[3] *the first month,* i.e. Nisan, usually April. Since it is difficult
to raise an army within a few weeks — Nicanor died in March —
it has been suggested that the year 152 (160) was a leap year
with an intercalated second month Ve-Adar or Adar Sheni.

[5f.] *Berea,* better "Birat," today El-Bireh, north of Jerusalem,
opposite *Elasa* (El-Ashshy).

a cause of reproach against our glory.' And the (Syrian) [11] host removed from the camp, and (the Jews) stood to encounter them; and the horse was divided into two companies, and the slingers and the archers went before the host together with all the mighty men that fought in the front. But Bacchides was on the right wing; and [12] the phalanx drew near from both sides, and they blew with their trumpets, and the men of Judah's side also blew with their trumpets; and the earth shook with the shout of the armies. And the battle was joined from [13] morning until evening. And when Judah saw that Bac- [14] chides and the main strength of his army were on the right wing, his followers concentrated their whole attention upon them, and the right wing was discomfited by [15] them and they pursued after them unto the mount Azotus. And when they that were on the left wing saw that [16] the right wing was discomfited, they turned and followed upon the footsteps of Judah and those that were with him. And the battle waxed sore, and many on [17] either side fell wounded to death. And Judah fell, and [18] the rest fled. And Jonathan and Simon took Judah their [19] brother, and buried him in the sepulchre of his fathers at Modin. And they bewailed him, and all Israel made [20] great lamentation for him and mourned many days, and said:

[15] *Azotus* cannot be Ashdod. Probably Mount Azor, today El Azur.

[16] The battle had turned in favor of Judah after his victory over the right wing. But the Syrian left wing attacked from the rear and defeated Judah.

[19] *took Judah their brother.* Either the Maccabees were able to rescue Judah's body or they received it by treaty from Bacchides (Josephus), before he was able to avenge Nicanor by mutilating it.

²¹ 'How is the mighty one fallen, the saviour of Israel!'
²² And the rest of the acts of Judah, and his wars, and the
valiant deeds which he did, and his greatness, — they
are not written; for they were exceeding many.

Jonathan's Succession
and Early Struggles

²³ And it came to pass after the death of Judah that the
lawless put forth their heads in all the borders of Israel,
²⁴ and all they that wrought iniquity rose up; in those days
there arose exceeding great murmuring that the land
²⁵ made peace with them. And Bacchides chose out the
²⁶ ungodly men and made them lords of the country. And
they sought out and searched for the friends of Judah,
and brought them to Bacchides, and he took vengeance
²⁷ on them, and treated them with mockery. And there was
great tribulation in Israel, such as was not since the time
²⁸ that a prophet appeared unto them. And all the friends
of Judah were gathered together, and they said unto
²⁹ Jonathan: 'Since thy brother Judah hath died, we have
no man like him to go forth against our enemies and Bacchides, and against them of our nation that are inimical
³⁰ to us. Now therefore we have chosen thee this day to be
our ruler and leader in his stead, that thou mayest fight

[21] From II Sam. 1:9 and Judg. 3:9.

[22] This concluding sentence resembles the one used for the
kings of Judah and Israel in the Book of Kings. — With Judah's
death major military victories came to an end. Many further
successes were achieved through the skilful use of the internal
discords of the Syrian Empire.

[23] Civil war flares up with new vigor, the Hellenists feeling
secure again. They find their match in Jonathan.

[27] *since the time that a prophet appeared to them* is a stylistic
phrase for the beginning of the Second Commonwealth (see

our battles.' And Jonathan took the leadership upon him ³¹
at that time, and rose up in the stead of his brother Judah.

And when Bacchides knew it, he sought to slay him. ³²
But when Jonathan, and Simon his brother, and all that ³³
were with him, knew it, they fled into the wilderness of
Tekoah, and encamped by the water of the pool Asphar.
And Bacchides got to know of this on the Sabbath day, ³⁴
and he came, he and all his army, over Jordan.
And (Jonathan) sent his brother, a leader of the multi- ³⁵
tude, and besought his friends, the Nabathaeans, that
they might leave with them their baggage, which was
much. But the children of Ambri came out of Medaba, ³⁶
and took John, and all that he had, and went their way
with it. But after these things they brought word to Jon- ³⁷
athan and Simon his brother, that the children of Ambri
were making a great marriage, and were bringing the
bride from Nadabath with a great train, a daughter of
one of the great nobles of Canaan. And they remembered ³⁸
John their brother, and went up, and hid themselves under the covert of the mountain; and they lifted up their ³⁹
eyes, and saw, and behold, a great ado and much baggage; and the bridegroom came forth, and his friends
and his brethren to meet the bridal procession with tim-
brels, and minstrels, and many weapons. And they rose ⁴⁰

4:46), when classical prophecy ceased, to be replaced by other
religious institutions.

[33] *Tekoah* was six miles south of Bethlehem; the reservoir
Asphar (Bir Ez-Za'feron), nine miles.

[34] is a misplaced duplicate of v.43.

[35] *Nabathaeans*, see 5:25.

[36] *the children of Ambri:* an Arab clan, living near *Medaba*,
southeast of the Jordan delta.

[37] *Nadabath*, or Nebo, a district northwest of Medaba. —
Canaan is the biblical name for pagan Palestine.

up from their ambush against them, and slew them; and
many fell wounded to death, and the rest fled into the
⁴¹ mountain; and they took all their spoils. And the marriage was turned into mourning, and the voice of their
⁴² minstrels into lamentation. And they avenged fully the
blood of their brother; and they turned back to the
marsh-land of Jordan.

⁴³ And when Bacchides heard it, he came on the Sabbath
⁴⁴ day unto the banks of the Jordan with a great host. And
Jonathan said unto his brethren: 'Let us arise now and
fight for our lives; for it is not with us as to-day, as yes-
⁴⁵ terday and the day before. For, behold, the battle is before us and behind us; moreover, the water of the Jordan
is on this side and on that side, and this is marsh- and
⁴⁶ wood-land, and there is no place to turn aside. Now,
therefore, cry unto heaven, that ye may be delivered out
⁴⁷ of the hand of your enemies.' And the battle was joined,
and Jonathan stretched forth his hand to smite Bac-
⁴⁸ chides, and he turned away back from him. And Jonathan, and they that were with him, leapt into the Jordan, and swam over to the other side; and Bacchides and
⁴⁹ his followers did not pass over Jordan against them. And
there fell of Bacchides' company that day about a thousand men.

⁵⁰ And they returned to Jerusalem; and they built strong
cities in Judaea, the stronghold that is in Jericho, and
Emmaus, and Bethhoron, and Bethel, and Timnath,
Pharathon, and Tephon, with high walls, and gates and

[50] Alarmed by Jonathan's strength, the Syrians created a
chain of fortifications: *Jericho,* near the Jordan delta; *Emmaus,*
see 3 : 40; *Bethhoron,* see 3 : 16; *Bethel,* ten miles north of Jerusalem; *Timnath,* thirteen miles northwest of Bethel; *Pharathon,*
southwest of Nablus-Shechem; *Tephon,* either Taphu in Samaria,
or Tappuach in Judea (location uncertain).

bars. And they set garrisons in them to vex Israel. [51]
And they fortified the city Bethsura, and Gazara, and [52]
the citadel; and they put forces in them, and store of
victuals. And they took the sons of the chief men of the [53]
country for hostages, and put them in ward in the citadel at Jerusalem.

Now in the one hundred and fifty-third year, in the sec- [54]
ond month, Alcimus commanded to pull down the wall
of the inner court of the sanctuary, in so doing he pulled
down also the works of the prophets. And when he began [55]
to pull down, at that time, Alcimus was stricken, and his
works were hindered; and his mouth was stopped, and
he became palsied, and he could no more speak anything, nor give order concerning his house. And Alcimus [56]
died at that time with great torment. And when Bacchi- [57]
des saw that Alcimus was dead, he returned to the king.
And the land of Judah had rest two years.

And all the lawless men took counsel, saying: 'Behold, [58]
Jonathan, and they of his part are dwelling at peace and
in security; let us therefore now bring Bacchides, and he
will lay hands on them all in one night.' And they went [59]
and consulted with him. And he removed, and came with [60]
a great host, and sent letters privily to all his confederates that were in Judaea, that they should lay hands on
Jonathan, and on them that were with him; but they
were not able to do so because their plan became known
to them. And they (that were of Jonathan's part) laid [61]
hands on about fifty men of the country that were the

[52] *Bethsura,* see 4 : 29, and *Gazara* (Gazera), see 4 : 15.

[54] *153* S.E. = 159 B.C.E. — *the wall of the inner court:* one of
the inner Temple walls, built with the sanction of the last prophets, separating Gentiles from Jews. Alcimus' tribute to the Hellenistic idea of the fraternization of nations threatened to efface
the difference between idolator and pious Jew.

⁶² ringleaders in the wickedness, and slew them. And Jona-
than, and Simon, and they that were with him, gat them
away to Bethbasi, which is in the wilderness, and he
built up that which had been pulled down thereof, and
⁶³ made it strong. And when Bacchides knew it, he gath-
ered together all his multitude, and sent word to them
⁶⁴ that were in Judaea. And he went and encamped against
Bethbasi, and fought against it many days, and made
⁶⁵ engines of war. And Jonathan left his brother Simon in
the city, and went forth into the country; and he went
⁶⁶ with a small number. And he smote Odomera and his
⁶⁷ brethren, and the children of Phasiron in their tents. And
he began to smite them and to go up with his troops.
Then Simon and they that were with him went out of the
⁶⁸ city and set on fire the engines of war; and they fought
against Bacchides, and he was discomfited by them, and
they afflicted him sore, for his plan and his attack had
⁶⁹ been in vain. And they were very wroth with the lawless
men that gave him counsel to come into the country, and
⁷⁰ they slew many of them. And he determined to depart
into his own land. And when Jonathan had knowledge
thereof, he sent ambassadors unto him, to the end that
they should make peace with him, and that he should
restore unto them the captives.
⁷¹ And he accepted, and did according to his words, and
sware unto him that he would not seek his hurt all the
⁷² days of his life. And he restored unto him the captives
which he had taken captive aforetime out of the land of

[62] *Bethbasi:* Chirbet Beit-Bassa, southeast of Bethlehem.

[66] The curbing of hostile Bedouin tribes fortifies Jonathan's
position.

[73] Jonathan has now become the head of a rival popular government for whose good will the claimants to the Syrian throne
are forced to contend. — *Michmash:* nine miles north of Jerusalem.

Judah; and he returned and departed into his own land, and came not any more into their borders. And the sword ⁷³ ceased from Israel. And Jonathan dwelt at Michmash. And Jonathan began to judge the people; and he destroyed the ungodly out of Israel.

Jonathan's Aid to a Syrian Revolution

In the one hundred and sixtieth year Alexander Epiph- ¹ anes, the son of Antiochus, went up and took possession of Ptolemais, and they received him, and he reigned there. And when king Demetrius heard thereof, he gathered to- ² gether exceeding great forces, and went forth to meet him in battle. And Demetrius sent letters unto Jonathan ³ with words of peace so as to magnify him. For he said: ⁴ 'Let us be beforehand to make peace with them, ere he makes peace with Alexander against us. For he will re- ⁵ member all the evils which we have done unto him, and unto his brethren and unto his nation.' And he gave him ⁶ authority to gather together forces, and to provide arms, and to be his confederate; and he commanded that they should deliver up to him the hostages that were in the citadel. And Jonathan came to Jerusalem, and read the ⁷ letters in the ears of all the people, and of them that were in the citadel; and they were sore afraid when they heard ⁸ that the king had given him authority to gather together forces. And they of the citadel delivered up the hostages ⁹ unto Jonathan, and he restored them to their parents.

[1] *160* s.e. = 153 b.c.e. Five years have elapsed since Bacchides' withdrawal.

Alexander Balas, a low-born Smyrnian who resembled Antiochus Eupator, pretended to be Antiochus Epiphanes' son. He was supported by Pergamum, Egypt and Rome, and by the dissatisfied Syrian populace.

Ptolemais, see 5:15.

[6] The army, conceded to Jonathan, was to be used as a Syrian unit.

¹⁰ And Jonathan dwelt in Jerusalem, and began to build
¹¹ and renew the city. And he commanded them that did
the work to build the walls and the mount Zion round
about with square stones for defence; and they did so.
¹² And the strangers, that were in the strongholds that
¹³ Bacchides had built, fled away; and each man left his
¹⁴ place, and departed into his own land. Only in Bethsura
were left certain of those that had forsaken the Law, and
the commandments; for it was a place of refuge unto
them.

¹⁵ And king Alexander heard all the promises which Demetrius had sent unto Jonathan; and they told him of
the battles and the valiant deeds which he and his
brethren had done, and of the toils which they had en-
dured; and he said: 'Shall we find another such man?
¹⁶ And now let us make him our Friend and confederate.'
¹⁷ And he wrote letters, and sent them unto him, according
¹⁸ to these words, saying: 'King Alexander to his brother
¹⁹ Jonathan, greeting! We have heard concerning thee,
that thou art a mighty man of valour, and meet to be our
²⁰ Friend. And now we have appointed thee this day high-
priest of thy nation, and (it is our will) that thou
shouldest be called the king's Friend' — and he sent

[11] *the walls,* which had been treacherously destroyed by Lysias, see 6:62.

[12f.] *strangers:* foreign mercenaries and merchants.

[20] *we have appointed thee . . . high-priest.* Precedents to such
appointments by the Syrians were those of Jason, Menelaus, and
Alcimus. In spite of this foreign "intervention," the religious
party seems temporarily to have approved of Jonathan's new
dignity, since he was their national liberator and of priestly
(though not high-priestly) origin. The legitimate dynasty had
officiated at the Jewish temple in Leontopolis in Egypt from the
time of their flight in 160.

[21] *the holy garment.* In pre-exilic times, investiture had taken

unto him a purple robe and a crown of gold — 'and that
thou shouldest take our part, and keep friendship with
us.' And Jonathan put on the holy garment in the sev- [21]
enth month of the one hundred and sixtieth year, at the
feast of Tabernacles and he gathered together forces,
and provided arms in abundance.

And when Demetrius heard these things, he was grieved, [22]
and said: 'Why have we permitted this to be done, that [23]
Alexander hath been beforehand with us in establishing
friendship with the Jews, to strengthen himself? I also [24]
will write unto them words of encouragement, and of
honour, and gifts, that they may be with me for aid.'
And he sent unto them according to these words: 'King [25]
Demetrius unto the nation of the Jews, greeting! Foras- [26]
much as ye have kept covenant with us, and have continued in our friendship, and have not joined yourselves
to our enemies, we, who have heard hereof, rejoice. And [27]
now continue ye still to keep faith with us, and we will
recompense unto you good things in return for what ye
do in our behalf; and we will grant you many immuni- [28]
ties, and will give you gifts. And now I free you, and re- [29]
lease all the Jews from the tributes, and from the custom on salt, and from (the presenting of) the crowns;

the place of anointing. That the people held the pontifical vest-
ments in great awe is evident from the legends which sprang up
about them and from the fact that some Roman procurators
seized them — a measure of political precaution.

   the feast of Tabernacles, i.e. Sukkot, commencing on the 15th
of Tishri (Sept./Oct.), 153 B.C.E.

[26] The letter purposely omits Jonathan in order to under-
mine his position.

[29] *the tributes* were a sliding scheme of poll tax; *salt* was an
important product of the environs of the Dead Sea; the *crowns:*
customary contributions to the royal coronation, developed into
a permanent crown tax.

³⁰ and instead of the third part of the seed, and instead of
the half of the fruit of the trees, which falleth to me to
receive, I release them from this day and henceforth,
so that I will not take them from the land of Judah, and
from the three governments which are added thereunto
from the country of Samaria and Galilee, from this day
³¹ forth and for all time. And let Jerusalem be holy and
free, together with the outlying districts, regarding the
³² tenths and the tolls. I yield up also my authority over
the citadel which is at Jerusalem, and give it to the high-
priest, that he may appoint in it such men as he shall
³³ choose, to keep it. And every soul of the Jews that hath
been carried away captive from the land of Judah into
any part of my kingdom, I set at liberty without price;
³⁴ and let all remit the tributes of their cattle also. And all
the feasts, and the Sabbaths, and new moons, and appointed days, and three days before a feast, and three
days after a feast, let them all be days of immunity and
³⁵ release for all the Jews that are in my kingdom; and no
man shall have authority to exact from any of them, or

[30] *the three governments* or toparchies, in southern Samaria.
They were administrative districts, centered around the towns of
Ephraim, Lydda and Ramathaim, with a largely Jewish population. — Omit *Galilee* as a scribal error. — *added thereunto:* here-
with given to Judea as a gift. The fact that Modin, the native
town of the Hasmoneans, was probably within the territory conceded to the Jews, made this transfer more desirable.

[31] *let Jerusalem be holy.* This refers to privileges granted by
Antiochus III: no pagan was to be admitted to the inner Temple
precincts, no meat of unclean animals brought into the city, and
all sacrifices offered in accordance with Jewish law. The status
of "holy and inviolable" (asyla) was granted to a number of
Hellenistic temple-cities in the 2nd cent. This privilege included
immunity from reprisal and war, the right of asylum, and tax
exemptions.

the tenths and the tolls. The Syrians had either taxed or seized

to trouble them concerning any matter. And let there ³⁶ be enrolled among the king's forces about thirty thousand men of the Jews, and pay shall be given unto them, as belongeth to all the king's forces. And of them some ³⁷ shall be placed in the king's great strongholds, and some of them shall be placed over the affairs of the kingdom, which are of trust; and let those that are over them, and their rulers, be from among themselves, and let them walk after their own laws, even as the king hath commanded in the land of Judah. And the three govern- ³⁸ ments that have been added to Judaea from the country of Samaria let them be added to Judaea, that they may be reckoned to be under one man, that they obey not any other authority than that of the high-priest. As for ³⁹ Ptolemais, and the land pertaining thereto, I have given it as a gift to the sanctuary that is at Jerusalem, for the expenses that befit the sanctuary. And I give every year ⁴⁰ fifteen thousand shekels of silver from the king's revenues, from the places which are convenient. And all the ⁴¹ overplus which the officials paid not in — as in former

the payments and gifts to the priests prescribed by the Torah as well as the annual Temple dues — one-third or one-half shekel — paid by all male Jews throughout the world.

[33] *captive.* The number of Jewish hostages and slaves must have been considerable after these numerous wars.

[34] *days of immunity and release* is explained by v.35.

[36f.] These are the obligations which the Jewish nation has to fulfil in exchange for the privileges granted to them.

[39] The gift of *Ptolemais* was an invitation to attack Alexander Balas, who was in possession of that city.

[40] *shekels:* a silver shekel was equivalent to an amount between fifty cents and a dollar, its actual buying power, however, being much higher.

[41] The Persians (536–332 B.C.E.), Egyptians (331–198), and

years — they shall from henceforth give towards the
⁴² work of the house. And beside this, the five thousand
shekels of silver, which they used to take from the dues
of the sanctuary out of the income year by year, this
also is released, because it appertaineth to the priests
⁴³ that minister. And whosoever shall flee unto the temple
that is in Jerusalem, and in all the precincts thereof, because he oweth money to the king, or for any other reason, let such go free, together with all, whatsoever they
⁴⁴ possess, in my kingdom. And for the building and renewing of the works of the sanctuary the expense shall be
⁴⁵ given also out of the king's revenue. And for the building of the walls of Jerusalem, and the fortifying thereof
round about, shall the expense be given also out of the
king's revenue, and for the building of the walls (of
other cities) in Judaea.'
⁴⁶ Now when Jonathan and the people heard these words,
they gave no credence unto them, nor received they
them, because they remembered the great evil that he
had done in Israel, and that he had afflicted them very
⁴⁷ sore. And they were well pleased with Alexander, because
he was the first that spake words of peace unto them,
and they remained confederate with him alway.
⁴⁸ And king Alexander gathered together great forces, and
⁴⁹ encamped over against Demetrius. And the two kings
joined battle, and the army of Alexander fled, and Demetrius followed after him, and prevailed against them.

Syrians up until Antiochus Epiphanes used to make regular contributions to the Temple. The king pretends that the payments
ceased because of the neglect of officials.

[43] It was Hellenistic policy to grant temple-cities the right to
grant asylum to all fugitives. The biblical law of asylum recognized six cities (see Exod. 21:14) as a refuge in the case of un-
premeditated manslaughter, and apparently, the altar of the
Jerusalem sanctuary in the cases of political crimes (I Kings
1:50).

And he continued the battle obstinately until the sun [50]
went down; and Demetrius fell that day.

And Alexander sent ambassadors to Ptolemy, king of [51]
Egypt, according to these words, saying: 'Forasmuch as [52]
I am returned to my kingdom, and am set on the throne
of my fathers, and have gotten the dominion, and have
overthrown Demetrius, and have gotten possession of
our country — yea, I joined battle with him, and he and [53]
his army were discomfited by us, and we sat upon the
throne of his kingdom, — let us now establish amity [54]
one with the other; and give me now thy daughter to
wife; and I will make affinity with thee, and will give
both thee and her gifts worthy of thee.' And Ptolemy [55]
the king answered, saying: 'Happy is the day wherein
thou didst return into the land of thy fathers, and didst
sit upon the throne of their kingdom. And now will I do [56]
according to the things which thou hast written. But
meet me at Ptolemais, that we may see one another; and
I will make affinity with thee even as thou hast said.'
And Ptolemy went out of Egypt, he and Cleopatra his [57]
daughter, and came unto Ptolemais, in the one hundred
and sixty-second year; and he bestowed on him his [58]
daughter Cleopatra, and celebrated her marriage at
Ptolemais with great pomp, as the manner of kings is.
And king Alexander wrote unto Jonathan, that he should [59]
come to meet him. And he went with pomp to Ptolemais, [60]
and met the two kings, and gave them and their Friends

[46] Considering Demetrius' character, Syria's inconsistent policy, and the Judean treaty with Rome (which also supported
Alexander), Jonathan was justified in his decision.

[51] *Ptolemy* VI Philometor, 180–146 B.C.E.

[52] *returned to my kingdom:* this falsehood was widely believed, by the author of our book, among others, see v.1.

silver and gold, and many gifts; and he found favour in
⁶¹ their sight. And there were gathered together against him
certain pestilent fellows out of Israel, men that were
transgressors of the Law to complain against him; but
⁶² the king gave no heed to them. And the king commanded,
and they took off Jonathan's garments, and clothed him
⁶³ in purple; even so did they do. And the king made him
sit with him, and said unto his princes: 'Go forth with
him into the midst of the city, and make proclamation,
that no man complain against him concerning any matter, and let no man trouble him for any manner of
⁶⁴ cause.' And it came to pass, when they that complained
against him saw his glory according as (the herald)
made proclamation, and saw him clothed in purple, that
⁶⁵ they all fled away. And the king showed him honour,
and wrote him among his Chief Friends, and made him
⁶⁶ a captain, and governor of a province. And Jonathan
returned to Jerusalem with peace and gladness.

⁶⁷ And in the one hundred and sixty-fifth year came De-
metrius, the son of Demetrius, out of Crete into the land
⁶⁸ of his fathers. And when king Alexander heard thereof
he was grieved exceedingly, and returned unto Antioch.
⁶⁹ And Demetrius appointed Apollonius, who was over
Coelesyria, captain; and he gathered together a great
host, and encamped in Jamnia, and sent unto Jonathan

[62] The *purple* was the symbol of his acquittal. Compare Mor-
decai's treatment, Esther 6 : 11ff.

[65] Since Jonathan had been made a "Friend" before (v.16),
the title *Chief Friend* indicates a promotion. — The military
(*captain*), civil (*governor*) and religious rule over Judea was now
in the hands of a traditional Jew. Yet the Syrian king still remained his sovereign.

[67] *165* s.e. = 147 b.c.e. — *Demetrius* II Nicator ("the con-
queror") rescued by his father *Demetrius* I and taken to Crete.

the high-priest, saying: 'Thou alone liftest up thyself [70]
against us; but I am had in derision and in reproach because of thee. And why dost thou vaunt thy power
against us in the mountains? Now therefore, if thou [71]
trustest in thy forces, come down to us in the plain, and
there let us try conclusions with one another, for with
me is the power of the cities. Ask and learn who I am, [72]
and the rest that help us; and they will say, Your foot
cannot stand before our face; for thy fathers have been
twice put to flight in their own land. And now thou wilt [73]
not be able to withstand the horse and such an host as
this in the plain, where there is neither stone nor flint,
nor any place to flee unto.' Now when Jonathan heard [74]
the words of Apollonius, he was moved in his mind; and
he chose out ten thousand men, and went forth from
Jerusalem; and Simon his brother met him for to help
him. And he encamped against Joppa; and they of the [75]
city shut him out, because Apollonius had a garrison in
Joppa; and they fought against it. And they of the city, [76]
being afraid, opened the gates. and Jonathan became
master of Joppa. And when Apollonius heard, he gath- [77]
ered an army of three thousand horse, and a great host,
and went to Azotus as though to journey on, but at the
same time moved forward into the plain, because he had
a multitude of horse, and relied on this. And he pursued [78]
after him to Azotus, and the armies joined battle. Now [79]

[69] *Coelesyria,* the "hollow of Syria," originally the land between the Lebanon mountains, included eastern Palestine and
Syria.

[72] *twice put to flight.* This seems to refer to early Jewish defeats by the Philistines in whose territory Apollonius' army was
massed (see I Sam. 4: 1ff.; 31: 1ff.).

[75] Jonathan wisely decided to establish contact with Ptolemy
and Alexander by occupying the important harbor of *Joppa*
(Jaffa).

Apollonius had left a thousand horse behind him, hidden; but Jonathan realized that there was an ambush-
⁸⁰ ment behind him. And they surrounded his army, and
cast darts at the people from morning until late in the
⁸¹ afternoon; but the people stood still, as Jonathan com-
⁸² manded, while the enemy's horses were wearying. And
Simon drew forth his host, and joined battle with the
phalanx — for the horsemen were spent — and they
⁸³ were discomfited by him, and fled. And the horsemen
were scattered in the plain; and they fled to Azotus, and
entered into Beth-dagon, their idol's temple, to save
⁸⁴ themselves. And Jonathan burned Azotus, and the cities
round about it, and took their spoils; and the temple of
Dagon, and them that fled into it, he burned with fire.
⁸⁵ And they that had fallen by the sword, with them that
⁸⁶ were burned, were about eight thousand men. And from
thence Jonathan removed, and encamped against Askalon, and they of the city came forth to meet him with
⁸⁷ great pomp. And Jonathan, with them that were on his
⁸⁸ side, returned to Jerusalem, having many spoils. And
it came to pass, when king Alexander heard these things,
⁸⁹ he honoured Jonathan yet more; and he sent unto him
a buckle of gold, as the use is to give to such as are of
the kindred of the kings; moreover, he gave him Ekron
and all the borders thereof for a possession.

[80] *his army,* i.e. Jonathan's.

[86] *Askalon:* one of the five chief cities of the Philistines between Ashdod and Gaza.

[89] *a buckle of gold:* the symbol of a further promotion.
    Ekron: between Ashdod and Jamnia, the northernmost of the
Philistine cities.

Jonathan's Statesmanship in the Wars for the Syrian Throne

And the king of Egypt gathered together great forces, 1
as the sand which is by the sea shore, and many ships,
and sought to make himself master of Alexander's kingdom by deceit, and to add it to his own kingdom. And he 2
went forth into Syria with words of peace; and they of
the cities opened unto him the gates, and met him, and
king Alexander's command was that they should meet
him, because he was his father-in-law. Now when Ptol- 3
emy entered into the cities, he placed in each city his
forces for a garrison. And when he came near to Azotus, 4
they showed him the temple of Dagon burned with fire,
and Azotus which together with the suburbs thereof,
had been pulled down, and the bodies scattered about,
and them that had been burned, whom he had burned
in the war, for they had made heaps of them in his way.
And they told the king what things Jonathan had done, 5
in order to cast blame on him; and the king held his
peace. And Jonathan met the king with pomp at Joppa, 6
and they saluted one another, and they slept there. And 7
Jonathan went with the king as far as the river that is
called Eleutherus, and returned to Jerusalem.
But king Ptolemy made himself master of the cities upon 8
the sea coast, unto Seleucia which is by the sea, and he

[1] *the king of Egypt* is the aforementioned Ptolemy Philometer,
10: 51. — *many ships.* Egypt was a strong naval power, which
maintained fleets in the Mediterranean and Red Sea.

[5] *the king held his peace,* because he could not afford to alien-
ate Jonathan.

[7] *Eleutherus,* today Nahr El-Kefir, north of Tripolis in Syria.

[8] *Seleucia which is by the sea:* so called in order to distinguish

⁹ devised evil devices concerning Alexander. And he sent
ambassadors unto king Demetrius, saying: 'Let us make
a covenant with one another, and I will give thee to wife
my daughter whom Alexander hath, and thou shalt reign
¹⁰ over thy father's kingdom; for I have repented that I
gave my daughter unto him, for he sought to slay me.'
¹¹ But he cast blame on him, because he coveted his king-
¹² dom. And taking his daughter (from Alexander) he gave
her to Demetrius, and was estranged from Alexander,
¹³ and their enmity became manifest. And Ptolemy entered into Antioch, and put on himself the diadem of
Asia; so he had put two diadems upon his head, the
diadem of Egypt and that of Asia.
¹⁴ But king Alexander was in Cilicia at that season, be-
¹⁵ cause they of those parts were in revolt. And Alexander
heard of it, and he came against him in war; and Ptolemy led forth his host, and met him with a strong force,
¹⁶ and put him to flight. And Alexander fled into Arabia,
that he might be sheltered there; but king Ptolemy was
¹⁷ exalted. And Zabdiel the Arabian took off Alexander's
¹⁸ head, and sent it to Ptolemy. And king Ptolemy died
the third day after; and they that were in his strongholds
¹⁹ were slain by them that dwelt in the strongholds. And
Demetrius became king in the one hundred and sixty-
seventh year.

it from a number of other cities with the name Seleucia, founded
by the Seleucid dynasty. Seleucia was the seaport of Antioch, the
capital.

[10] *he sought to slay me.* According to Josephus, Alexander
tried to have his father-in-law killed by his minister Ammonius.

[13] *Asia:* in this case a term for Coelesyria, Phoenicia, and
Eastern Asia Minor. Ptolemy could not annex more territory for
fear of Rome.

[14] *Cilicia,* a province in Asia Minor.

[17] *Zabdiel* was the chieftain of an Arab tribe south of Damascus.

In those days Jonathan gathered together them of Ju- [20] daea to take the citadel that was in Jerusalem; and he made many engines of war against it. And certain ones [21] that hated their own nation, men that transgressed the Law, went unto the king, and reported unto him that Jonathan was besieging it, and that he should meet him [22] and speak with him at Ptolemais with all speed. But [23] when Jonathan heard this he commanded that the citadel should continue to be besieged; and he chose certain of the elders of Israel and of the priests and put himself in peril, and taking silver and gold and rai- [24] ment, and divers presents besides, went to Ptolemais unto the king. And he found favour in his sight. And [25] certain lawless men of them that were of the nation made complaints against him; but the king did unto him [26] even as his predecessors had done unto him, and exalted him in the sight of all his Friends, and confirmed him [27] in the high-priesthood, and whatsoever other honours he had before, and gave him pre-eminence among his Chief Friends. And Jonathan requested of the king, [28] that he would make Judaea and the three provinces of the country of Samaria free from tribute, and he promised him three hundred talents. And the king consented, [29] and wrote letters unto Jonathan concerning all these things after this manner:

[18] *Ptolemy died.* After he had been mortally wounded in battle, the Syrians annihilated the remaining Egyptian garrisons.

[19] *167 s.e.* = 145 b.c.e. *Demetrius'* reign further weakened the Syrian Empire, which at that time lost Media to Parthia.

[26] Jonathan's position was now so strong that in spite of Hellenistic-Jewish intrigues and of his siege of Acra, he had to be received with favor.

[29] *three hundred talents* (about $120,000) : it was not clearly stated whether this sum had to be paid annually or only once in compensation for a complete release of taxes (the latter being equivalent to the sale of the taxation right). This ambiguity led to further conflict.

³⁰ 'King Demetrius unto his brother Jonathan and unto
³¹ the nation of the Jews, greeting; The copy of the letter
which we wrote unto Lasthenes our kinsman concerning you, we have written also unto you, that ye may see.
³² King Demetrius unto Lasthenes his father, greeting;
³³ We have determined to do good to the nation of the Jews,
who are our friends, and observe what is just toward us,
³⁴ because of their good will toward us. We have confirmed
unto them, therefore, the districts of Judaea, and the
three governments of Aphaerema, and Lydda, and Ramathaim — these were added unto Judaea from the
country of Samaria — and all things appertaining unto
them, for all such as do sacrifice in Jerusalem, instead of
the king's dues which the king received of them yearly
aforetime from the produce of the land and the fruits of
³⁵ trees. And as for the other things which appertain unto
us, from henceforth, of the tenths and the tolls that appertain to us, and the saltpits, and the crowns that
³⁶ appertain to us, all these we will bestow upon them. And
not one of these things shall be annulled from this time
³⁷ forth and for ever. Now therefore be careful to make a
copy of these things, and let it be given unto Jonathan,
and let it be set upon the holy mount in a fitting and
conspicuous place.'

³⁸ And when king Demetrius saw that the land was quiet
before him, and that no resistance was made to him, he
sent away all his forces, each man to his own place, —
except the foreign forces, which he had raised from the
isles of the Gentiles — and therefore all the forces of his

[31f.] *kinsman* is, like *father*, v.32, an honorary title.

[34] *Aphaerema:* Ephraim, see 10:30. — *as do sacrifice in Jeru-*
salem, i.e. Jews, for Samaritans sacrificed on Mt. Garizim.

[37] There is no mention of the Syrian Acra, the siege of which
probably had to be lifted.

fathers were inimically disposed towards him. Now Try- 39
phon was of those who aforetime had been of Alexander's part, and he saw that all the forces murmured
against Demetrius, and he went to Imalkue the Arabian,
who was nourishing up Antiochus, the young child of
Alexander, and pressed sore upon him that he should 40
deliver him unto him, that he might reign in his father's
stead; and he told him all that Demetrius had done, and
the hatred wherewith his forces hated him; and he abode
there many days.

And Jonathan sent unto king Demetrius, that he should 41
cast out of Jerusalem them of the citadel and them that
were in the strongholds; for they fought against Israel
continually. And Demetrius sent unto Jonathan, saying: 42
'I will not only do this for thee and thy nation, but I will
greatly honour thee and thy nation, if I find favourable
occasion. Now therefore thou shalt do well, if thou send 43
me men who shall fight for me; for all my forces are re-
volted.' And Jonathan sent him three thousand valiant 44
men unto Antioch. And they came unto the king; and
the king was glad at their coming. And they of the city 45
gathered themselves together into the midst of the city,
to the number of a hundred and twenty thousand men;
and they were minded to slay the king. And the king fled 46
into the palace, and they of the city seized the thorough-
fares of the city, and began to fight. And the king called 47
the Jews to aid, and they were gathered unto him all at
once; and they dispersed themselves in the city; and
they slew that day to the number of a hundred thousand.
And they set the city on fire, and got many spoils that 48

[39] *Imalkue* may have been the successor of Zabdiel, v.17.

[45] These figures as well as those of v.47 are stylistic exaggera-
tions.

[47f.] The Jews fought together with the king's mercenaries.

⁴⁹ day, and saved the king. And when they of the city saw
that the Jews had made themselves masters of the city
as they would, they waxed faint in their hearts, and
⁵⁰ cried out to the king with supplication, saying: 'Give us
thy right hand, and let the Jews cease from fighting
⁵¹ against us and the city.' And they cast away their arms,
and made peace. And the Jews were glorified in the sight
of the king, and before all that were in his kingdom; and
⁵² they returned to Jerusalem, having many spoils. And
when king Demetrius was seated on his throne of his
⁵³ kingdom again, and the land was quiet before him, he
lied in all that he had spoken, and estranged himself
from Jonathan and recompensed him not according to
the benefits with which he had promised to recompense
him; but he afflicted him sore.

⁵⁴ Now after this Tryphon returned, and with him the
young child Antiochus; and he reigned, and put on a dia-
⁵⁵ dem. And there were gathered unto him all the forces
which Demetrius had sent away in disgrace; and they
⁵⁶ fought against him, and he fled, and was put to rout. And
Tryphon took the elephants, and became master of Anti-
⁵⁷ och. And the young Antiochus wrote unto Jonathan,
saying: 'I confirm unto thee the high-priesthood, and
appoint thee over the four governments, and to be one of
⁵⁸ the king's Friends.' And he sent unto him golden vessels
and furniture for the table, and gave him leave to drink

[53] *recompensed him not:* Demetrius tried to enforce again the
old system of tributes, see v.29.

[54] *Antiochus,* the sixth of this name, Epiphanes Dionysus.

[57] *the four governments:* Judea and the three governments
mentioned in v.34.

[59] *Ladder of Tyre:* a mountainous district, fourteen miles
north of Ptolemais.

[61] *Gaza* is the southernmost of the five Philistine cities.

in golden vessels and to be clothed in purple, and to have a golden buckle. And his brother Simon he made governor from the Ladder of Tyre unto the borders of Egypt. 59 And Jonathan went forth, and took his journey beyond 60 the river and through the cities; and all the forces of Syria gathered themselves unto him for to be his confederates. And he came to Askalon, and they of the city 61 met him honourably. And he departed thence to Gaza, and they of Gaza shut him out; and he lay siege unto it, and burned the suburbs thereof with fire, and spoiled them. And they of Gaza made request unto Jonathan, 62 and he gave them his right hand, and took the sons of their princes for hostages, and sent them away to Jerusalem. And he passed through the country as far as Damascus.

And Jonathan heard that Demetrius' princes were come 63 to Kedesh, which is in Galilee, with a great host, with the object of hindering him from his purpose; and he 64 went to meet them, but Simon his brother he left in the country. And Simon encamped against Bethsura, and 65 fought against it many days, and shut it up; and they 66 made request to him that he would give them his right hand, and he gave it to them; but he put them out from thence, and took possession of the city, and set a garrison over it. And Jonathan and his army encamped at the 67 water of Gennesar, and early in the morning they got them to the plain of Hazor. And, behold, an army of 68

[62] *Damascus:* 120 miles northeast of Jerusalem.

[63] *Kedesh:* on the northern frontier of Palestine, in the Book of Joshua a Levitical center and city of refuge (Josh. 21:32).

[65] *Bethsura,* see 4:29, one of the remaining Syrian strongholds in Judea.

[67] *water of Gennesar* (-eth) or Kinneret: the Sea of Galilee. *the plain of Hazor:* near Lake Merom (Hule).

strangers met him in the plain, and they laid an ambush
for him in the mountains, but they themselves met him
⁶⁹ face to face. But they that lay in ambush rose out of
their places, and joined battle; and all they that were
⁷⁰ of Jonathan's side fled; not one of them was left, except
Mattathias the son of Absalom, and Judah the son of
⁷¹ Chalphi, captains of the forces. And Jonathan rent his
⁷² clothes, and put earth on his head, and prayed. And he
turned again unto them in battle, and put them to rout,
⁷³ and they fled. And when they of his side who were flee-
ing saw it, they returned unto him, and pursued with
him unto Kedesh to their camp; and they encamped
⁷⁴ there. And there fell of the strangers on that day about
three thousand men. And Jonathan returned unto Jerusalem.

Jonathan's Successful Foreign Policy

¹ And Jonathan saw that the time served him, and he
chose men, and sent them to Rome, to confirm and re-
² new the friendship that they had with them. And to the
Spartans, and to other places, he sent letters after the
³ same manner. And they went unto Rome, and entered
into the senate house, and said: 'Jonathan the high-
priest, and the nation of the Jews, have sent us, to renew

[70] These two valiant captains remained with their units, fifty
men, according to Josephus.

[74] Jonathan was thus able to keep his country free from in-
vasions during the time of the Syrian wars of succession.

[5] Jonathan's diplomatic skill reveals itself in his choice of *the
Spartans,* who were the nation least implicated in the great Greek
(Achean) revolt against Rome and permitted to retain much of
their sovereignty (146 B.C.E.). Even if not all details of the document are authentic, it is, nevertheless, probable that there was a
friendly exchange of correspondence between Judea and Sparta.

for them the friendship and the confederacy, as in former time.' And they gave them letters unto the governors of every place, that they should bring them on their way to the land of Judah in peace. And this is the copy of the letter which Jonathan wrote to the Spartans: 'Jonathan the high-priest, and the Council of the nation, and the priests, and the rest of the people of the Jews, unto their brethren the Spartans, greeting! Even before this time were letters sent unto Onias the high-priest from Areios, who was reigning among you, that ye are our brethren, as the copy here underwritten showeth. And Onias treated honourably the man that was sent, and received the letters, wherein declaration was made of confederacy and friendship. Therefore we also — albeit we need none of these things, having for our comfort the holy books which are in our hands — have assayed to send that we might renew our brotherhood and friendship with you, to the end that we should not become estranged from you altogether; for long time is passed since ye sent unto us. We therefore at all times without ceasing, both at our feasts, and on other convenient days, do remember you in the sacrifices which we offer, and in our prayers, as it is right and meet to be mindful of brethren; and moreover, we are glad for your glory. But as for ourselves, many afflictions and many wars

[6] *The Council of the nation,* somewhat later called Sanhedrin (Heb., from the Greek synedrion, "gathering"), exercised some legislative and judicial power. The higher priesthood, the lay aristocracy and later, the scribal party, were represented in it.

[7] *Onias* I was high priest until about 300 B.C.E., Onias II somewhat later; both were contemporaries of *Areios* I, 309–265 B.C.E.

[9] *our comfort:* the records of victories and the prophecies of consolation.

   holy books. Practically all the books of the Bible were in existence at that time.

have encompassed us, and the kings that are round
14 about us have fought against us. We were not minded,
however, to be troublesome to you, or to the rest of our
15 confederates and friends, in these wars; for we have the
help that is from heaven to help us, and we have been
delivered from our enemies, and our enemies have been
16 humiliated. We chose, therefore, Numenius the son of
Antiochus, and Antipater the son of Jason, and have sent
them unto the Romans, to renew the friendship that we
17 had with them, and the former confederacy. We commanded them, therefore, to go also unto you, and to
salute you, and to deliver you our letters concerning the
18 renewing of friendship and of our brotherhood. And
now ye shall do well if ye give us an answer thereto.'
19 And this is a copy of the letters which they sent to Onias:
20 'Areios, king of the Spartans, to Onias, the chief priest,
21 greeting! It hath been found in writing concerning the
Spartans and the Jews, that they are brethren, and that
22 they are of the stock of Abraham; and now, since these
things have come to our knowledge, ye shall do well to
23 write unto us of your prosperity. And we, moreover, do
write on our part to you, that your cattle and goods are
ours, and ours are yours. We do command, therefore,
that they make report unto you on this wise.'

[16] *Antipater the son of Jason,* probably the son of the former
ambassador to Rome, see 8:17. Diplomacy seems to have been,
much as it is today, the task of a professional "caste."

   unto the Romans. Jonathan skilfully alludes to his friendship
with Rome.

[19] It is probable that this Spartan letter is a well-meant Judean invention. In a similar vein, the Romans claimed that
Romulus and Remus were of Greek descent. In Asiatic cities
similar legends were current. See v.21.

[21] *brethren.* The idea of the brotherhood of nations was widespread in the time of Hellenism. There was a Greek tradition
tracing the origin of the Greeks back to the Phoenicians (the

And Jonathan heard that Demetrius' princes were re- 24
turned to fight against him with a greater force than
afore, so he removed from Jerusalem, and met them in 25
the country of Hamath; for he gave them no respite
to set foot in his country. And he sent spies into their 26
camp; and they returned, and reported unto him that
in such and such a way they had planned to fall upon
him by night. But as soon as the sun was down, Jona- 27
than commanded his men to watch, and to be in arms,
that all the night long they might be ready for battle;
and he sent forth sentinels round about the camp. But 28
when the adversaries heard that Jonathan and his men
were ready for battle, they were afraid and trembled
in their heart; and they kindled fires in their camp, and
departed. But Jonathan and his men knew it not till 29
morning; for they saw the fires burning. And Jonathan 30
pursued after them, but did not overtake them; for they
had gone over the river Eleutherus. And Jonathan turned 31
aside against the Arabians, who are called Gabadaeans,
and smote them, and took their spoils. And he set out 32
from thence, and came to Damascus, and took his journey through all the country.

And Simon went forth, and took his journey as far as 33
Askalon, and the strongholds that were near unto it. And

close neighbors and relatives of the Jews), and a Jewish tradition which found friendly nations in the genealogical lists of
Genesis (such as Gen. 10–11; 25; 36).

[24] These events took place immediately after Demetrius' withdrawal from northern Palestine, see 11 : 74.

[25] *Hamath,* today Hama, on the Orontes, a city and its environs, north of the Palestinian frontier, see Num. 13 : 21.

[30] The *Eleutherus* (11 : 7) seems to have formed the frontier
between Phoenicia and Syria.

[31] The *Gabadaeans* (or Zabadeans) must have lived close to
Damascus. Jonathan fought them as vassal of Antiochus VI.

34 he turned aside to Joppa, and took possession of it, for he had heard that they were minded to deliver the stronghold unto the men of Demetrius; and he placed a garrison there to keep it.

35 And Jonathan returned, and called the elders of the people together; and he took counsel with them to build strongholds in Judaea, and to make the walls of Jerusa-
36 lem higher, and to raise a great mound between the citadel and the city, for to separate it from the city, so that it might be isolated, that they within it might neither
37 buy nor they without sell. And they were gathered together to build the city; and a part of the wall by the brook that is on the east side had fallen down, and he
38 repaired that which is called Chaphenatha. And Simon also built Adida in the plain country, and made it strong, and set up gates and bars.

39 And Tryphon sought to reign over Asia and to put on himself the diadem, and to stretch forth his hand against
40 Antiochus the king. And he was afraid lest haply Jonathan should not suffer him, and lest he should fight against him; so he sought a way how to take him, that
41 he might destroy him. And he removed, and came to Bethshan. And Jonathan came forth to meet him with forty thousand men chosen for battle, and came to Beth-
42 shan. And when Tryphon saw that he came with a great host, he was afraid to stretch forth his hand against him;
43 and he received him honourably, and commended him unto all his Friends, and gave him gifts, and commanded his Friends and his forces to be obedient unto him, as
44 unto himself. And he said unto Jonathan: 'Why hast thou put all this people to trouble, seeing there is no war
45 betwixt us? And now, send them away to their homes,

[37] *Chaphenatha.* The significance of this term is unknown. If it is an Aramaic name for the mound (one MS.), it may mean "hunger wall."

but choose for thyself a few men who shall be with thee, and come thou with me to Ptolemais, and I will give it up to thee, and the rest of the strongholds and the rest of the forces, and all the officers; then I will return and depart; for, for this cause did I come.' And he trusted him and 46 did even as he said, and sent away his forces, and they departed into the land of Judah. But he reserved to him- 47 self three thousand men, two thousand of whom he left in Galilee, but one thousand went with him. But when Jon- 48 athan had entered into Ptolemais, they of Ptolemais shut the gates, and took him; and all they that had come with him they slew with the sword. And Tryphon sent forces 49 and horsemen into Galilee, and into the great plain, to destroy all Jonathan's men. And they perceived that he 50 was taken and had perished, and they that were with him; nevertheless they encouraged one another, and went on their way close together, ready for war. And 51 when they that were following upon them saw that they were ready to fight for their lives, they turned back again. And they all come in peace to the land of Judah, 52 and they mourned for Jonathan and them that were with him, and they were sore afraid. And all Israel mourned 53 with a great mourning. And all the Gentiles that were round about them sought to destroy them utterly, for they said: 'They have not a man that is leader and who will help them; now therefore let us fight against them, and take away their memorial from among men.'

Progress toward National Sovereignty under Simon

And Simon heard that Tryphon had gathered together a 1 a numerous host to come into the land of Judah, and to

[38] *Adida,* near Lydda, in the coastal plain (Shefelah).
[1] It was left for Simon, the last survivor of the five Maccabean brothers, to hasten the liberation and pacification of Judea.

² destroy it utterly. And he saw that the people were troubled and in great fear; so he went up to Jerusalem, ³ and gathered the people together, and encouraged them, and said unto them: 'Ye yourselves know what things I, and my brethren, and my father's house, have done for the laws and the sanctuary, and the battles and the dis- ⁴ tresses which we have seen; by reason whereof all of my brethren have perished for Israel's sake, and I alone am ⁵ left. And now be it far from me that I should spare my own life in any time of affliction; for I am not better than ⁶ my brethren. Howbeit I will take vengeance for my na- tion, and for the sanctuary, and for our wives and chil- dren; because all the Gentiles are gathered together to ⁷ destroy us of very hatred.' And the spirit of the people, ⁸ as soon as they heard these words, revived. And they an- swered with a loud voice, saying: 'Thou art our leader ⁹ instead of Judah and Jonathan thy brethren. Fight thou our war, and all that thou shalt say unto us, that will we ¹⁰ do.' And he gathered together all the men of war, and made haste to finish the walls of Jerusalem, and fortified ¹¹ it round about. And he sent Jonathan the son of Absa- lom, and with him a great host, to Joppa; and he cast out them that were therein, and abode there in it.

¹² And Tryphon removed from Ptolemais with a mighty host to enter into the land of Judah; and Jonathan was ¹³ with him in ward. But Simon encamped at Adida, over ¹⁴ against the plain. And when Tryphon knew that Simon

[4] *all my brethren have perished:* Simon was unaware that Jonathan was still alive.

[6] *the Gentiles are gathered together.* The presence of the pagan populations of rural Palestine, her large Greek cities, as well as the hostile tribes across her borders, rendered the existence of little Judea ever precarious.

[10] *finish the walls of Jerusalem,* completing Jonathan's work (12:36f.).

was risen up instead of his brother Jonathan, and meant
to join battle with him, he sent ambassadors unto him,
saying: 'It is for the money which Jonathan thy brother 15
owed unto the king's treasure, by reason of the offices
which he had, that we hold him fast. And now send a hun- 16
dred talents of silver, and two of his sons as hostages,
that when he is set at liberty he may not revolt from us,
— and we will set him at liberty.' And Simon knew that 17
they spake unto him deceitfully, but sent the money and
the children, lest peradventure he should bring upon
himself great hatred on the part of the people, in that 18
they should be saying: 'Because I sent him not the
money and the children he perished.' And he sent the 19
children and the hundred talents; and he dealt falsely
and did not set Jonathan at liberty. And after this Try- 20
phon came to invade the land, and destroy it, and he
went round about by the way to Adora; and Simon and
his army marched over against him to whatsoever place
he went. Now they of the citadel sent unto Tryphon am- 21
bassadors, hastening him to come unto them through the
wilderness, and to send them victuals. And Tryphon 22
made ready all his horse to come; and in that night there
fell a great quantity of snow, and he did not come because of the snow; so he removed, and came into the
country of Gilead. But when he came near to Bascama, 23
he slew Jonathan, and he was buried there. And Tryphon 24
returned, and went away into his own land.

[11] *Joppa* was already in Jewish hands. However, *he cast out*
the unreliable Philistine element in order to safeguard this vital
port, which remained Jewish thereafter.

[13] *Adida,* see 12 : 38.

[20] *Adora* (Adoraim, Dura), near Hebron. Simon always
moved between the enemy and Jerusalem, carefully watching
Tryphon's advance.

[23] *Bascama* (Tell Bazuk), near the Sea of Galilee. — The

²⁵ And Simon sent, and took the bones of Jonathan his brother, and buried him at Modin, the city of his fathers.
²⁶ And all Israel made great lamentation over him, and
²⁷ mourned for him many days. And Simon built (a monument) upon the sepulchre of his father and of his brethren, and raised it aloft, so that it could be seen from afar;
²⁸ with polished stone behind and before. And he set up seven pyramids, one over against another, for his father,
²⁹ and mother, and four brethren. And for these he made cunning devices, setting about them great pillars, and upon the pillars he fashioned all manner of arms for a perpetual memory, and beside the arms carved ships,
³⁰ that they should be seen of all that sail on the sea. This is the sepulchre which he made at Modin, and it is there unto this day.

³¹ Now Tryphon dealt deceitfully with the young king
³² Antiochus, and slew him, and reigned in his stead, and put on himself the diadem of Asia, and brought great calamity upon the land.
³³ And Simon built the strongholds of Judaea, and fenced

Latin version of our book reads: *he slew Jonathan* and his sons.

[28] *seven pyramids,* the seventh being reserved for Simon himself.

[29] *carved ships.* If the text is in order, the ships must have symbolized Judea's new naval aspirations after the acquisition of Joppa. — It is probable that the Hasmonean burial place was an imitation of the Seleucid sepulchers on top of the cliffs of Seleucia.

they, i.e. the pillars and their crests. *should be seen:* they stood on a hilltop and were visible from the sea, twelve miles distant.

[30] *until this day,* i.e. the time of the author of I Maccabees. The last mention of the sepulcher as extant is in a 4th-cent. Christian work.

them about with high towers, and great walls, and gates, and bars; and he laid up victuals in the strongholds. And 34 Simon chose men, and sent to king Demetrius, to the end he should give the country an immunity, because all that Tryphon did was to plunder. And king Demetrius sent 35 unto him according to these words, and answered him, and wrote a letter unto him, after this manner: 'King 36 Demetrius unto Simon the high-priest and Friend of kings, and unto the elders and nation of the Jews, greeting. The golden crown, and the palm-branch, which ye 37 sent, we have received; and we are ready to conclude a lasting peace with you, and to write to the officers to grant immunities unto you. And whatsoever things we 38 have now confirmed unto you, they are confirmed; and the strongholds which ye have builded, let them be your own. As for any oversights and faults committed unto 39 this day, we forgive; and the crown which ye owed (we remit); and if there were any other toll exacted in Jerusalem, let it no longer be exacted. And if there be some of 40 you meet to be enrolled among those round about us, let them be enrolled; and let there be peace betwixt us.' In 41

[31] The mention at this point of the murder of Antiochus VI (by bribed physicians) offers chronological difficulties.

[36ff.] This document was found to be so important that the author reproduces it in its original wording.

[37] The *palm-branch* (probably shaped like a scepter) was a symbol of strength in the Scriptures (Ps. 92:12); of peace, in the Hellenistic world.

[39] *oversights and faults:* the disputed tributes which had not been paid.

[41] *177* S.E. = 142 B.C.E. The fall of the remaining Syrian fortresses probably preceded this "declaration of independence," see v.43, "in those days."

the one hundred and seventieth year was the yoke of the
⁴² heathen taken away from Israel. And the people of Israel
began to write in their instruments and contracts: 'In
the first year of Simon the great high-priest and captain
and leader of the Jews.'

⁴³ In those days he encamped against Gazara, and compassed it round about with armies; and he made an engine of siege, and brought it up to the city, and smote one
⁴⁴ tower, and took it. And they that were in the engine of
⁴⁵ siege leaped forth into the city; and there was a great
uproar in the city; and they of the city rent their clothes,
and went up on the wall with their wives and children,
and cried with a loud voice, making request to Simon to
⁴⁶ give them right hands. And they said: 'Deal not with us
according to our wickedness, but according to thy
⁴⁷ mercy.' And Simon was reconciled unto them, and did
not fight against them; but he drove them out of the
city, and cleansed the houses wherein the idols were, and
⁴⁸ so entered into it with singing and giving of praise. And
he put all uncleanness out of it, and caused to dwell in it
men who observed the Law; and he made it stronger
than it was before, and he built therein a dwelling-place
for himself.

yoke of the heathen. Judea was not occupied nor tributary any
longer, but still bound to enroll troops in the Syrian army.

[42] *the first year:* in honor of Simon a new era was inaugurated.
Earlier Jewish systems of chronology were based on the exodus
from Egypt, the erection of Solomon's Temple, and the accession
of native or foreign kings (see also 14:27). In the Hellenistic
period, many Greek cities proclaimed a new era upon their liberation from imperialistic rule.

high-priest . . . captain . . . leader. Like his brother Jonathan
before him, Simon was the religious (and judicial), military, and
political head of the nation.

[43] *Gazara,* see 9:52.

But they of the citadel of Jerusalem were hindered from 49
going forth, and from going into the country, and from
buying and selling; and they hungered exceedingly, and
many of them perished through famine. And they cried 50
out to Simon to take right hands; which thing he granted
them; but he cast them out from thence; and he cleansed
the citadel from pollutions. And he entered into it on the 51
three and twentieth day of the second month, in the one
hundred and seventy-first year, with praise, and palm-
branches, and with harps and cymbals, and with viols
and with hymns, and with songs; because a great enemy
had been destroyed out of Israel. And he ordained that 52
they should keep that day every year with gladness. And
the hill of the temple that was by the citadel he made
stronger; and he dwelt there, he and his men. And Simon 53
saw that John his son was grown to be a man, and he
made him leader of all his forces; and he dwelt at Gazara.

Simon's Exalted Rank
at Home and Abroad

In the one hundred and seventy-second year Demetrius 1
the king gathered his forces together, and went into

[51] The date is the 23rd of Iyyar, 141 B.C.E.

[52] *every year.* This memorial feast was observed for some
time, as Megillat Taanit, the "Scroll of Fasting," shows. This
scroll, compiled in the beginning of the Common Era, consists of
a list of festivals on which fasting was prohibited.

[53] *John:* Simon's successor (134–103 B.C.E.), surnamed Hyrcanus because of his military service on the Parthian front in
Hyrcania.

[1] *172* S.E. = 140 B.C.E. — *Media* is the country south of the
Caspian Sea.

Media, to get him help, that he might fight against Try-
2 phon. And when Arsaces, the king of Persia and Media,
heard that Demetrius was come into his borders, he sent
3 one of his leaders to take him alive; and he went and
smote the army of Demetrius, and took him, and
brought him to Arsaces; and he put him in ward.

4 And the land had rest all the days of Simon; and he
sought the good of his nation; and his authority and his
5 glory was well-pleasing to them all his days. And in addition to all his glory he took Joppa for a haven, and
made it a place of entry for the ships of the sea.
6 And he enlarged the borders of his nation,
    And ruled over the land.
7 And he gathered together many that had been in cap-
    tivity,
        And he ruled over Gazara, and Bethsura, and the
        citadel.
    And he took away uncleannesses therefrom,
        And there was none that could resist him.
8 And they tilled their land in peace;
        And the land gave her increase,
    And the trees of the plains their fruit.
9   Old men sat in the streets,
    All spoke together of the common weal,
        And the young men put on glorious and warlike ap-
        parel.
10 For the cities he provided victuals,
        And furnished them with defensive works.

[2] *Arsaces* is the dynastic name of the Parthian (neo-Persian)
kings. The monarch in question was Mithridates I, 171–138 B.C.E.,
who had invaded the eastern provinces of Syria. Demetrius was
forced to fight him before turning against Tryphon.

[4] The ode on Simon's achievements appears to commence with
v.4, not v.6. It is full of biblical phrases, especially from Zech. 8.

Until his glorious name was proclaimed to the end of
the earth.

He made peace in the land,   11
And Israel rejoiced with great joy.

And each sat under his vine and his fig tree,   12
And there was none to make them afraid;

And no one was left in the land to fight them   13
And the kings were discomfited in those days.

And he strengthened all that were brought low of his   14
people;
He sought out the Law,

And put away the lawless and the wicked.
He glorified the sanctuary.   15

And multiplied the vessels of the Temple.

And when it was heard in Rome that Jonathan was dead,   16
and even unto Sparta, they were exceeding sorry. But as   17
soon as they heard that his brother Simon was made
high-priest in his stead, and ruled the country, and the
cities therein, they wrote unto him on tablets of brass,   18
to renew with him the friendship and the confederacy
which they had established with Judah and Jonathan his
brethren; and they were read before the congregation in   19
Jerusalem. And this is the copy of the letter which the   20
Spartans sent: 'The rulers and the city of the Spartans,
unto Simon the high-priest, and unto the elders, and the
priests, and the rest of the people of the Jews, brethren,
greeting; The ambassadors that were sent unto our   21
people made report to us of your glory and honour; and

[8] The picture drawn of the ideal peace and prosperity is chiefly
agricultural, reflecting the economic state of Judea at that time.

[16–24] These verses offer some difficulties. Vv. 16–23 would
seem to be an interpolation. Some scholars read v.24 before vv.
16–23. In this case Numenius would have sent messengers to
Jerusalem and remained in Rome (see 15:15).

²² we were glad for their coming. And we did register the
things that were spoken by them in the public records,
after this manner: Numenius, son of Antiochus, and An-
tipator, son of Jason, the Jews' ambassadors, came unto
²³ us to renew the friendship they had with us. And it
pleased the people to receive the men honourably, and to
place the copy of their words among the public records,
to the end that the people of the Spartans might have a
memorial thereof.' Moreover they wrote a copy of these
²⁴ things unto Simon the high-priest. After this Simon sent
Numenius to Rome having a great shield of gold of a
thousand pound weight, in order to confirm the confederacy with them.

²⁵ But when the people heard these things, they said:
²⁶ 'What thanks shall we give to Simon and his sons? For
he, and his brethren, and his father's house have made
themselves strong, and have chased away in fight the
enemies of Israel from them, and established liberty for
²⁷ it.' And they wrote on tablets of brass and set them upon
a pillar in mount Zion. And this is the copy of the writing: 'On the eighteenth day of Elul, in the one hundred
and seventy-second year — that is the third year of
Simon the high-priest, and the prince of the people of
²⁸ God — in a great congregation of priests and people and
princes of the nation, and of the elders of the country,
²⁹ the following was promulgated by us; Forasmuch as

[24] Omit the word *weight*, according to the Syriac version.
a thousand pound refers to the value (about $30,000).

[27] *172* S.E. = 140 B.C.E. Note that the Seleucid chronology (in
the Talmud, "Era of the Contracts") is still in use. It maintained
itself among European Jews until the 13th cent., after which the
counting from the creation of the world gradually replaced it.
Yemenite Jews still use it.

[28] *prince of the people of God*. The Syriac version reads "the

oftentimes there have been wars in the country, Simon
the son of Mattathias, the son of the children of Joarib,
and his brethren, put themselves in jeopardy, and with-
stood the enemies of their nation, that their sanctuary
and the Law might be upheld; and they glorified their
nation with great glory. And Jonathan assembled their 30
nation together, and became high-priest to them; and he
was gathered to his people. Then their enemies deter- 31
mined to invade their country, that they might destroy
their country utterly, and stretch forth their hands
against their sanctuary. Then rose up Simon and fought 32
for his nation; and he spent much of his own substance,
and armed the valiant men of his nation, and gave them
wages. And he fortified the cities of Judaea, and Beth- 33
sura upon the borders of Judaea, where the arms of the
enemies were aforetime, and set there a garrison of Jews.
And he fortified Joppa which is by the sea, and Gazara 34
which is upon the borders of Azotus, wherein the enemies
dwelt aforetime; and he placed Jews there, and whatsoever things were needful for the sustenance of these he
put in them. And when the people saw the faith of Simon, 35
and the glory which he sought to bring unto his nation,
they made him their leader and high-priest, because he
had done all these things, and because of the justice and
the faith which he kept to his nation, and because he
sought by all means to exalt his people. And in his days 36
things prospered in his hands, so that the Gentiles were

prince of Israel," which sounds less artificial and is in line with
the habit of the author to avoid the mention of the Deity.

priests and people: read "priests of the people" instead.

princes of the nation: probably members of the Sanhedrin,
ministers and generals.

elders of the country: probably magistrates and heads of clans.

[29f.] Judah is not mentioned by name, since the document deals
with the office of high priest.

taken away out of their (the Jews') country; and they
also that were in the city of David, they that were in
Jerusalem, who had made themselves a citadel, out of
which they issued, and polluted all things round about
the sanctuary, and did great hurt unto its purity, these
37 did he expel; and he made Jews to dwell therein, and
fortified it for the safety of the country and of the city;
38 and he made high the walls of Jerusalem. And king Demetrius confirmed him in the high-priesthood in conse-
39 quence of these things, and made him one of his Friends,
40 and honoured him with great honour. For he had heard
that the Jews had been proclaimed by the Romans
friends, and confederates, and brethren, and that they
41 had met the ambassadors of Simon honourably. And the
Jews and the priests were well pleased that Simon should
be their leader and high-priest for ever, until a faithful
42 prophet should arise; and that he should be a captain
over them, to set them over their works, and over the
country, and over the arms, and over the strongholds,
and that he should take charge of the sanctuary, and that
43 he should be obeyed by all, and that all instruments in
the country should be written in his name, and that he
44 should be clothed in purple, and wear gold; and that it
should not be lawful for anyone among the people or
among the priests to set at nought any of these things,
or to gainsay the things spoken by him, or to gather an
assembly in the country without him, or that any other
45 should be clothed in purple or wear a buckle of gold; but
that whosoever should do otherwise, or set at nought any

[41] *a faithful prophet:* a trustworthy, truly inspired prophet,
who would authorize this enactment or decide differently.

[47] The title "king" is not used. Judea was still within the
framework of the Syrian Empire. Moreover, orthodox Jews considered only Davidides as legitimate aspirants to royalty.

[49] *the treasury* was a group of buildings and included the
archives.

of these things, should be liable to punishment. And all 46
the people consented to ordain for Simon that it should
be done according to these words. And Simon accepted, 47
and consented to fill the office of high-priest, and to be
captain and governor of the Jews and of the priests, and
to preside over all matters.

And they commanded to put this writing on tablets of 48
brass, and to set them up within the precinct of the sanctuary in a conspicuous place; and copies of this to be
placed in the treasury, to the end that Simon and his sons 49
might have them.

New Clashes with Syria

And Antiochus, son of Demetrius the king, sent letters 1
from the isles of the sea unto Simon the priest and governor of the Jews, and to all the nation; and the contents 2
thereof were after this manner: 'King Antiochus to
Simon the high-priest and governor, and to the nation of
the Jews, greeting: Forasmuch as pestilent fellows have 3
made themselves masters of the kingdom of our fathers,
and my purpose is to claim the kingdom, that I may restore it as before, — I have, moreover, raised a multitude of foreign soldiers, and have prepared ships of war, 4
and I have determined to land in the country, that I may
punish them that have devastated our country, and them
that have made many cities in the kingdom desolate, —
I therefore confirm unto thee the release from all the ex- 5
actions which the kings that were before me remitted

[1] *Antiochus* VII, *son of Demetrius* I, brother of the captive
Demetrius II, surnamed Sidetes ("from Side," see v.22).

the isles of the sea: he departed from Rhodes.

sent letters. He needed all the support he could muster, since the
combined power of the Parthians and Tryphon was considerable.

[5] The new concession made in this document is the right to
strike coins. — The fact that preceding treaties were always made

unto thee, and whatsoever gifts besides they remitted
⁶ unto thee; and I give thee leave to coin money for thy
⁷ country with thine own stamp. And Jerusalem and the
sanctuary shall be free; and all the arms which thou
hast prepared, and the strongholds which thou hast
built, which thou hast in thy possession, let them remain
⁸ unto thee. And everything owing to the king, and the
things that shall be owing to the king, let them be re-
⁹ mitted unto thee from now and unto all time. Moreover,
when we shall have established our kingdom, we will
glorify thee and thy nation and the Temple with great
glory, so that your glory shall be made manifest in all the
earth.'

¹⁰ In the one hundred and seventy-fourth year Antiochus
went forth into the land of his fathers; and all the forces
came together unto him, so that there were few men with
¹¹ Tryphon. And king Antiochus pursued him, and in flee-
¹² ing he came to Dor, which is by the sea; for he perceived
that troubles were come upon him, and that his forces
¹³ had forsaken him. And Antiochus encamped against
Dor, and with him a hundred and twenty thousand men
¹⁴ of war, and eight thousand horse. And he compassed the

the basis for new ones accounts for the stereotyped text of these
documents.

[10] *174* s.e. = 139/138 b.c.e.

[11] *Dor* or Tantura, an old seaport close to Caesarea.

[16] From Josephus it becomes probable that this document was
written under Hyrcanus II, 68–40 b.c.e., and was inserted here
thereafter, although a certain *Lucius* (Calpurnius Piso) actually
was consul in 139.

   Ptolemy VII, Euergetes Physkon, 170–117 b.c.e.

[21] *pestilent fellows.* Exiled members of the anti-Maccabean
party were still dangerously active abroad.

   fled from their country unto you. Egypt, owing to her proxim-
ity to Palestine, was the favorite haven for political refugees

city round about, and the ships joined in the attack from
the sea; and he pressed the city sore by land and sea, and
suffered no man to go out or in.

And Numenius and his company came from Rome, hav- 15
ing letters to the kings, and to the countries, wherein
were written these things:
'Lucius, consul of the Romans, unto king Ptolemy, 16
greeting: The Jews' ambassadors came unto us as our 17
friends and confederates, to renew the old friendship
and confederacy, being sent from Simon the high-priest,
and from the people of the Jews; moreover, they brought 18
a shield of gold of a thousand pound. It pleased us, there- 19
fore, to write unto the kings and unto the countries, that
they should not seek their hurt, nor fight against them,
and their cities, and their country, nor be confederates
with such as fight against them. And it seemed good to us 20
to accept the shield from them. If, therefore, any pesti- 21
lent fellows should have fled from their country unto
you, deliver them unto Simon the high-priest, that he
may take vengeance on them according to their law.'
And the same things wrote he to Demetrius the king, and 22
to Attalus, and to Ariarathes, and to Arsaces, and unto 23

from Solomon's time on (I Kings 12:2; Jer. 42; 43).

[22] This letter was sent to several countries of Asia Minor, and
to important cities and islands in the Mediterranean.

King *Attalus* II of Pergamum, 159–138; *Ariarathes* V of Cap-
padocia, 162–131 (Asia Minor); *Arsaces,* see 14:2. *Sampsames:*
probably a Black Sea port, if not an error for Lampsacus, a port
opposite Gallipoli. *Delos, Samos, Rhodes* and *Cos:* islands off the
coast of Asia Minor; *Myndos, Halicarnassus* and *Cnidus:* cities
of *Caria,* on the southwest coast of Asia Minor; *Sicyon:* a Greek
harbor which prospered after the destruction of Corinth; *Pamphylia* (main harbor: *Side*), *Lycia* (harbor: *Phaselis*): countries on the coast of Asia Minor; *Aradus:* an island off Phoenicia; *Gortyna:* a town on Crete; *Cyrene:* the capital of Libya
(North Africa).

all the countries, and to Sampsames, and to the Spartans, and unto Delos, and unto Myndos, and unto Sicyon, and unto Caria, and unto Samos, and unto Pamphylia, and unto Lycia, and unto Halicarnassus, and unto Rhodes, and unto Phaselis, and unto Cos, and unto Side, and unto Aradus, and Gortyna, and Cnidus, and Cyprus ²⁴ and Cyrene. And a copy hereof they wrote to Simon the high-priest.

²⁵ And Antiochus the king encamped against Dor the second day, bringing his forces up to it continually, and making engines of war; and he shut up Tryphon from ²⁶ going in or out. And Simon sent him two thousand chosen men to fight for him, and silver and gold, and instru- ²⁷ ments of war in abundance. But he would not receive them, but set at nought everything he had previously covenanted with him; and he was estranged from him. ²⁸ And he sent unto him Athenobius, one of his Friends, to commune with him, saying: 'Ye hold possession of Joppa and Gazara, and the citadel that is in Jerusalem, ²⁹ cities of my kingdom. The borders thereof have ye wasted, and done great hurt in the land, and have got ³⁰ the dominion of many places in my kingdom. Now, therefore, deliver up the cities which ye have taken, and the tributes of the places whereof ye have gotten do- ³¹ minion outside of the borders of Judaea; or else give me for them five hundred talents of silver; and for the harm that ye have done, and the tributes of the cities,

[25] The meaning of this passage, which continues 15:11ff. (the siege of Dor; 15:15-24 being an interlude), becomes clear by translating the abrupt Greek of this verse by "(to say this) *a second* (time)" instead of *"on the second* (day)."

[27] *was estranged.* This estrangement may have been brought about by the Roman letter to Demetrius, or by the influence of older Syrian officials and the pagan populations of the district.

other five hundred talents; otherwise we will come and make war upon you.' And when Athenobius, the king's [32] Friend, came to Jerusalem, and saw the glory of Simon, and the cabinet with gold and silver vessels, and his great attendance, he was amazed, and reported to him the king's words. And Simon answered, and said unto [33] him: 'We have neither taken other men's land, nor have we possession of that which appertaineth to others, but of the inheritance of our fathers; howbeit, it was had in possession of our enemies wrongfully for a certain time. But we, having the opportunity, hold fast the inher- [34] itance of our fathers. Nevertheless, as touching Joppa [35] and Gazara which thou demandest, — they that did great harm among the people and in our land — we will give a hundred talents for them.' And he answered [36] him not a word, but returned in a rage to the king, and reported unto him these words, and the glory of Simon, and all things whatsoever he had seen; and the king was exceeding wroth.

But Tryphon embarked on board a ship, and fled to Or- [37] thosia. And the king appointed Cendebaeus chief captain of the sea-coast, and gave him forces of foot and horse; and he commanded him to encamp before Ju- [39] daea; also he commanded him to build up Kedron, and to fortify the gates, and that he should fight against the people; but the king pursued Tryphon. And Cende- [40] baeus came to Jamnia, and began to provoke the people, and to invade Judaea, and to take the people cap-

[32] The display of riches had a similarly fateful effect in Isa. 39 : 2-6 (Hezekiel and the Babylonian embassy).

[37] *Orthosia:* on the Phoenician coast.

[39] *chief captain of the sea-coast:* military governor of Philistea and Phoenicia, the key territories to the Judean hill country.
    Kedron: today Katra near Modin.
    Tryphon fled to Apamea in Syria in order to make a stand

⁴¹ tive and to slay them. And he built Kedron, and set
horsemen there, and forces of foot, to the end that, is-
suing out, they might make outroads upon the ways of
Judaea, according as the king had commanded him.

¹ And John went up from Gazara, and told Simon, his
² father, what Cendebaeus was doing. And Simon called
his two eldest sons, Judah and John, and said unto them:
'I and my brethren and my father's house have fought
the battles of Israel from our youth, even unto this
very day; and things have prospered in our hands, so
³ that we were able to deliver Israel oftentimes. But now
I am old, and ye, moreover, by (God's) mercy, are of
sufficient age; be ye instead of me and my brother, and
go forth and fight for our nation; and let the help that
⁴ is from Heaven be with you.' And he chose out of the
country twenty thousand men of war and horsemen;
and they went against Cendebaeus, and rested at Modin.
⁵ And rising up in the morning, they went into the plain,
and, behold, a great host came to meet them, of footmen
and horsemen; and there was a brook betwixt them.
⁶ And he encamped over against them, he and his people;
and he saw that the people were afraid to pass over the
brook, so he passed over first; and when the men saw
⁷ him, they passed over after him. And he divided the
people, and set the horsemen in the midst of the footmen, for the enemies' horsemen were exceedingly nu-
⁸ merous. And they sounded with the trumpets; and Cen-

against Antiochus, but was defeated and forced to commit suicide.

[2] *Judah and John.* A third son, Mattathias, is mentioned in
v.14.

[7] *the horsemen in the midst.* This unusual strategy counter-
balanced the numerical superiority of the enemy. This is the first
appearance of Hasmonean cavalry, apparently organized during
the breathing-spell of Simon's reign.

debaeus and his army were put to the rout, and there
fell of them many wounded to death; and they that
were left fled to the stronghold. At that time was Judah,   9
John's brother, wounded; but John pursued after them,
till he came to Kedron, which (Cendebaeus) had built.
And they fled unto the towers that are in the fields of   10
Azotus; and he burned it with fire; and there fell of
them about a thousand men. And he returned to Judaea
in peace.

Simon's End and John's Accession

And Ptolemy the son of Abubus had been appointed   11
captain for the plain of Jericho; and he had much silver and gold, for he was the high-priest's son-in-law.   12
And his heart was lifted up, and he was minded to make   13
himself master of the country; and he took counsel deceitfully against Simon and his sons, to make away with
them. Now Simon was visiting the cities that were in   14
the country, and taking care for the good ordering of
them. And he went down to Jericho, he himself and Mattathias and Judah, his sons, in the one hundred and
seventy-seventh year, in the eleventh month, the same
is the month Shevat. And the son of Abubus received   15
them deceitfully into the little stronghold that is called
Dok, which he had built; and he made them a great
banquet; and he hid men there. And when Simon and   16
his sons had drunk freely, Ptolemy and they that were

[8] *the stronghold:* Kedron, see 15:39.

[11] *the son of Abubus.* He was Simon's son-in-law.

[14] *177* S.E. = 135 B.C.E. *Shevat,* Jan./Feb.

[15] The traitor did not dare to execute his plan in the open
city of Jericho but went to the nearby fortress of *Dok.*

[16] A similar incident is reported in I Kings 16:9f., when king
Elah was murdered by Zimri.

with him rose up, and took their arms, and came upon
Simon into the banqueting hall, and slew him and his
17 two sons, and certain of his servants. And he committed
a great act of treachery, and recompensed evil for good.
18 And Ptolemy wrote these things, and sent to the king,
that he should send him forces to aid him, and that he
19 should deliver to him their country and the cities. And
he sent others to Gazara to make away with John; and
unto the captains of thousands he sent letters to come
unto him that he might give them silver and gold and
20 gifts. And others he sent to take possession of Jerusalem,
21 and of the mount of the Temple. And one ran before to
Gazara, and told John that his father and brethren had
perished, 'and,' said he, 'he hath sent to slay thee also.'
22 And when he heard it, he was sore amazed; and he laid
hands on the men that came to destroy him, and slew
them; for he perceived that they were seeking to destroy
him.
23 And the rest of the acts of John, and of his wars, and
of his valiant deeds which he did, and of the building of
24 the walls which he built, and of his other deeds, behold
they are written in the chronicles of his high-priesthood,
from the time that he was made high-priest after his
father.

[22] John was able to enter Jerusalem before Ptolemy and quell
the rebellion after a siege of Jericho. He lost however his captive
mother, whom Ptolemy executed before his flight.

[23] Some of *the walls* of Jerusalem had to be razed in accordance with a truce with Antiochus VII Sidetes after renewed heavy
fighting. John I Hyrcanus rebuilt them in 129, the year of Antiochus' death, which marked the end of the Seleucid Empire as a
great power and brought the fulfilment of the aspirations of the
Jewish people after forty years of hardship.

[24] *the chronicles:* see 9:22. These official annals are lost.
   high-priest, see 13:53. His son, Aristobulos I, 104–103, assumed the title of king.

Chronology and Maps

Chronology

330: Alexander the Great conquers Palestine.

3rd Century: Palestine under the Ptolemies of Egypt.

200: Antiochus III of Syria conquers Palestine.

176: Antiochus IV Epiphanes.

169: First Egyptian campaign of Epiphanes. The Temple plundered.

168: Second Egyptian campaign. Founding of Acra.

167: Temple desecrated; beginning of the persecutions.

166: Uprising of Mattathias.

165: Judah succeeds to the leadership. Lysias' campaign.

164: End of the persecution. Epiphanes' amnesty.

Temple dedication. Inauguration of Hanukkah.

163: Death of Epiphanes. Campaign of Eupator. Defeat of Judah.

162: Treaty of peace. Alcimus high priest.

161: Judah's victory over Nicanor. Alliance with Rome.

160: Death of Judah.

159: Death of Alcimus.

152: Jonathan high priest.

146: Destruction of Corinth by the Romans.

142: Death of Jonathan. Simon.

141: Conquest of Acra.

140: Simon ethnarch.

134: Death of Simon.

134–104: John Hyrcanus I.

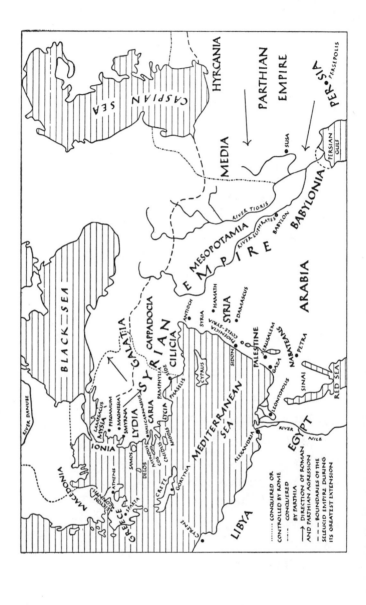

PALESTINE AND SYRIA IN
MACCABEAN TIMES

10   20
          MILES